Stick Around

Strategies to keep your gym members motivated
and maximise member revenue

Guy Griffiths

A catalogue record for this book is available from the British Library

ISBN 978-1-291-18537-9

Published by GG Fit Ltd
Web: www.ggfit.com
Email: info@ggfit.com
Tel: 020 7612 7531

Distributed by Lulu
Web: www.lulu.com

Acknowledgements

I would like to thank all my friends and family for help and encouragement as I wrote this book.

To all clients, partners, and associates of GG Fit, thanks for your time, I hope that this book helps you to give your members and clients more time, health and fitness.

Particular credit goes to Penelope Tobin who badgered me into getting started with Stick Around, Sylvia Worth for her fine editing toothcomb, and Kate Burton for coaching me through the final stages.

And most of all, thanks to my wife Tracy for her constant support and unwavering belief in me and in GG Fit.

Contents

1. Introduction

About this book

The purpose of this book is directly aligned with the mission of GG Fit: to help as many people as possible to be healthier and fitter by motivating them to exercise more.

Working with clubs has been our best route to this goal so far. It is expected that *Stick Around* will help to spread the message and reach out to more people working in the fitness industry, and increase understanding of what works for member retention.

It is widely known that member retention is a problem in the fitness industry, but only a few people are focusing on doing something about it and, even then, with mixed results. Some clubs are pleased with 12-month retention rates of around 50 per cent, but in any other industry, to lose half of your customers every year would be disastrous. As a result, many clubs choose to focus on sales, but this usually just exacerbates the problem.

This book looks at processes, techniques and initiatives that you can implement in your club to start improving your member retention today.

It is split into four main sections: journey, people, communication and systems. Part 1 looks at the member journey in detail, while Part 2 considers people, communication and systems. You can choose to jump back and forth, or start by focusing on one area. There are many cross-references throughout. For example, a low-cost club with a low/no staff model may focus less on people and more on communication. A leisure trust might look to review its journey and systems first, and move onto communication later.

Much of the book is written with retention systems in mind, but it also covers how systems work, and how to build a very simple retention system.

Like GG Fit, the book focuses on retaining members rather than new member sales. It also does not cover the 'obvious' customer service aspects of running a gym such as cleaning, well-serviced equipment, or the fitness knowledge or qualifications of staff. These are taken as given. If your club is dirty, you don't need a book or consultant to tell you how to fix it.

If you feel that you could use some help with implementing the ideas in this book, or managing the change process, then please contact us through www.ggfit.com

---

If you're looking to make a change in your club, or in anything else in business or life, it is worth bearing in mind the following change formula:

Change happens when:

$$Co\ (SQ) > R\ (C)$$

Your challenge is to decipher the formula before reading Chapter 10 (Conclusion), where all will be revealed.

Three cornerstones of great retention

Although this book first explores the member journey, this is more to link the processes and set out the picture for the 3-core parts of good member retention, namely people, communication and systems as shown in the diagram below.

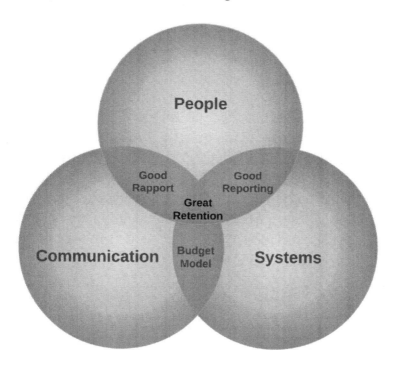

Core parts of good member retention

Good member retention can happen when any two of the above parts are present, but for really great results, a balance between all three parts is required.

People

People are traditionally the biggest influence on member retention. A club needs good staff that welcome and interact with members in the club, building up rapport and recording information about members to help them to reach their goals. When staff are focused on helping all your members to get results, the positive outcomes will be reflected in the club's retention rates.

Communication

Communication is sometimes seen as the new (less traditional) route to retain members. This is because SMS/text, e-mail and social media platforms are relatively new channels, but we have been communicating for many years face to face, by letter, and telephone. Using the right channels for your members and your club is key, as is getting a balance between the different methods in appropriate circumstances. This way, your members receive just the right amount of communication.

Systems

Put very simply, systems are tools that enable staff to store and retrieve data. Information that is recorded about members, such as their BMI, goals, gym visits, programme, and so on, acts as a prompt when contacting the member, and can trigger reminders or rewards. Even if a fitness instructor has a fantastic memory, storing information in their head doesn't benefit other staff. It is useful to aggregate all member data in order to report on retention rates, and identify areas for improvement.

Contracts

The view from outside the fitness industry is that contracts *are* the retention policy for many clubs. The new budget clubs with their 'no crazy annual contract' pledges are great for the industry, and are winning market share with their fresh approach.

Contracts favour sales staff, who can guarantee a commission if they can ensure that a member pays for at least 12 months. Other than that, contracts are just a lazy way of getting members to stay (and/or pay) for the length of the contract.

Gyms will hopefully focus less on contracts in the future

Signing members up to a 12-month contract can give false promise to the 12-month retention rate; say 60 per cent stay for 12 months, there may be a sharp fall in the number of members in month 13 and 14. Length of membership, based on number of visits rather than payment, is a good alternative indicator of member engagement. See Chapter 9 (Systems) for more information about the various reporting systems.

There is a place for using contracts in the fitness industry as an option for members to perhaps get a reduced rate (as do annual up-front agreements). At the end of the day, offering choice is a good thing.

Having a no-contract (or monthly) option can actually improve retention, since the club works harder to retain these members, and is less lackadaisical about members cancelling.

This book does not discuss contracts as retention tools.

Segmentation

There's more on segmentation in Chapter 8 (Communication), but it's useful to mention it here as part of the introduction too, in order to understand the member's journey better.

Segmenting members into groups is useful if you want to treat different members in various ways. It can bring more focus to your retention initiatives, make them more effective, and save time and money.

A very simple segmentation might be 'active' and 'inactive' members, where active members are those who have visited in the last 30 days, and the rest are inactive. You might decide to send your newsletter only to active members, for example.

It is good practice to keep segmentation as simple as possible. Too many differing levels of segmentation can lead to very detailed groups of members, or even individuals in each segment, which can make things complex. Clubs sometimes segment based on membership types, but unless you want to distinguish between different membership types in order to treat them differently, this is unnecessary.

The table below gives some examples of member segments that are too detailed, as you are unlikely to communicate or treat all the different groups differently. These are compared or combined into more manageable segments.

Too many segments	Practical Segments
New – Annual	
New – Monthly 12	New – Contract
New – Monthly 1	
New – PAYG	New – P&P
New – Offer	
Existing – Annual	
Existing – Monthly	Existing members
Existing – PAYG	

Segmentation examples

Segmentation is a useful tool when you want to offer members more attention; for example, in the early stages of their membership. New members should be a focus for staff, and within the new member segment, you might focus even more on new inexperienced members, or members who have returned from absence (churned members).

The diagram below shows the proportion of new members and their composition as experienced, inexperienced or churned members. Looking at your chart can be a useful exercise simply to find out the relative proportions and decide whether you want to combine any segments that are too detailed or small.

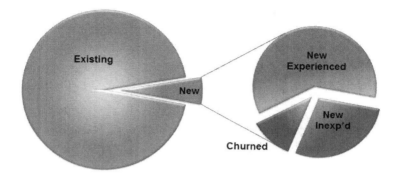

New and existing members

Summary

Whether you read this book from cover to cover, focus on one section, or use it as a reference, we hope that it will help you to get your members to stick around for longer, make them fitter, healthier and happier, and help the bottom line of your business too. Please feedback any comments, ideas, or requests through www.ggfit.com, where you can find all our contact details.

PART 1

The Member Journey

2. New member journey

At many clubs, the new member journey *is* the journey; a month or two after joining, the member may begin to attend the gym less frequently or stop altogether and 'fall off the radar'. To boost retention and the member's fitness, the journey needs to continue onward, which will be described in Chapter 3.

The new member part of the journey covers: joining; choices and options (for the member and the club); timescales; and tracking or measurement.

Joining

The journey starts before the member joins. You should collect information about the prospect over and above that given in the Physical Activity Readiness Questionnaire (PAR-Q) (see below) from their very first point of contact, visit or call. Knowing whether a new member has previous gym experience and what their goals or exercise aspirations are can enable you to you tailor their journey. Members who are new to exercise will benefit from more 'hand-holding' through their first weeks, whereas more experienced members might like the option of a fast-track induction.

Talking about the new member's exercise goal(s) is a good way of finding out more about them, and checking on their motivational needs early in their membership. Some people question whether sales staff should talk to members about their goals, but there's no harm in asking if a member has a goal. As long as no unreasonable promises are made about achieving the goal, this is a great sales technique. Setting a SMART (Specific, Measurable, Achievable, Relevant and Timely) goal for a member is the fitness professional's responsibility, as they will be helping to define the exercise programme, and motivating the member moving forward. If you want to read more about goal setting, jump forward to Chapter 7 (Interaction) now.

Member data

Collecting member data seems straightforward, but you can make it easier by incorporating it into your existing processes.

Add a couple of fields to your enquiry form, or an extra question to the PAR-Q. If the joining process is online, add a mandatory question to the sign-up form, and tell your members why you want this information. Making it easier for the member to complete the form/ provide information is also important; multiple choice options help, although for goals, you might consider using free text or require a SMART statement (this makes it harder, but helps later on in the member's journey).

To really find out about your members and prospects, you could use a tool like Technogym's Club 2.0 aspiration finder, which shows what 'moves' them from the six core aspirations. These are: sport, power, shape, move, balance and fun. See Chapter 9 (Systems) for more information.

Physical Activity Readiness Questionnaire

The PAR-Q, or Physical Activity Readiness Questionnaire, is a standard document that most clubs require new members to complete. Some are filled in online, others on paper. The PAR-Q typically asks a series of 'fit for exercise' questions, referring the member to medical advice if there are any anomalies.

Additional questions can be added to the PAR-Q to discover more about your new members. Examples are shown below.

PAR-Q questions

How much exercise have you done before?

   a) Very little
   b) Some, not recently
   c) Lots

What do you want to achieve at the club? For example, I'd like to feel and look fitter; I want to fit into my old jeans; I want to be able to run 10km in under 1hour.

Online joining question:
Tell us about your previous exercise experience:

   a) Not much to tell
   b) I used to exercise regularly
   c) I've always trained regularly

Beware of creating too many options; this can make tracking the journey complex. A 'one size fits all' minimal journey is simpler to manage, although you will have more members who don't comply with it (usually the more experienced ones). However, tailoring the journey will be more effective in terms of overall retention, and you will be providing a more bespoke service to your members.

Choices and options

There are various options available for new members, depending on their previous experience, as shown in the diagram below. These may include a one-2-one induction; taking part in a group induction; or proceeding to activities in the gym without an induction.

Members who are new to the gym have one 'choice' whereas experienced members have a full choice of all three options.

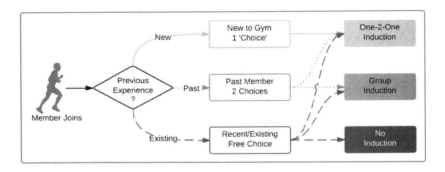

New member joining options

Remember that sometimes the journey will end before the member joins! However, if you have collected information such as previous experience, goals, or aspirations, then you can use this in future mailings to your prospect, for example telling prospects about your new absolute beginners' classes or latest offer.

Timescales

How long will the new member journey last? This needs to be defined so that you (and your members) know when they progress from being a 'fresher' to a regular member. The new member time frame varies from a couple of weeks to three months, depending on the resources, club size, and number of steps in the journey.

Again, you could vary the length of the new member journey based on previous experience, but this adds another level of complexity, and would make measurement more difficult. Most clubs use a standard time frame for everyone. If some members complete the initial journey quicker, so be it. If less experienced members need to extend, or even repeat, their new journey, this does not present a problem.

Journey steps

Next you need to decide how many steps your new member journey will have. There is no magic number that works for all clubs, or even different types of clubs. A good starting point is the rate that new members join and the staff resources you have to deal with them. It's no good aiming to spend five one-hour sessions with each new member in their first month if it's not possible. Keep it manageable, and give the customer what they need, or want, if you can by offering options. An example of a new member's journey is shown in the diagram below.

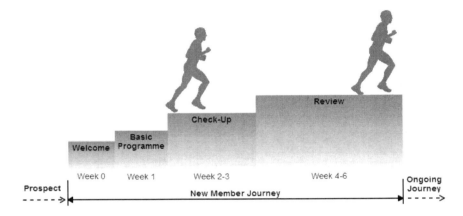

Example of a new member journey

Explain the route to the new member, so they know what to expect and when. This can even be used as part of the sales pitch; for example, 'this is how we keep your motivation levels up'. Some clubs are moving away from terms such as 'induction' or 'appointment' and using 'welcome' or 'getting started'. Make sure everyone (members and staff) know how long each step should take: is it up to an hour, a half-hour, or just a 5-minute chat, or touch base? (a touch base is often used as a very quick interaction; 'How's your training going?', 'Fine thanks' that takes a few seconds). And after each step, remind yourself and the member when the next contact will be, especially at the end of the new member journey.

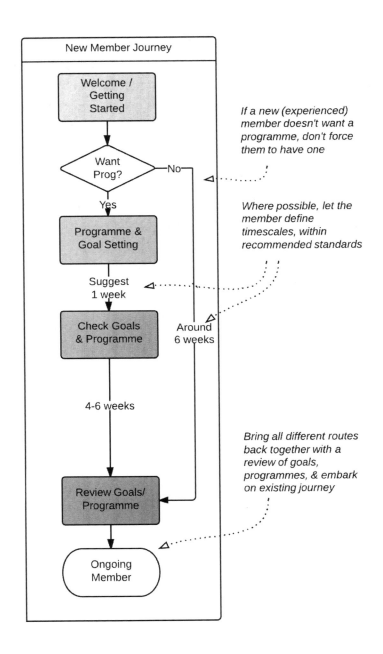

New member journey flowchart

If changing the naming convention of your member journey, keep it within your brand, perhaps soften the terms if you or your members don't like 'inductions', and make it easy to measure and follow. But overall, make it appealing to your members; it is in their interest that they follow it through to completion, as they will stay longer and be fitter!

Measure

'If you don't measure it, you can't improve it.' Lord Kelvin

Keeping the journey simple is important so that you can measure its success. At the very least, you should be able to monitor how many members complete the new member journey; a simple percentage score (and target) can feedback performance to staff and management. If you use different journey options, compare the length of membership, drop-out rate, or retention between the different journeys, and adapt or adjust accordingly, just as you would with pricing.

In the new member steps journey example (shown on page 28), it is straightforward to count how many 'Welcomes', 'Basic Programmes', 'Check-Ups' and 'Reviews' are performed on a monthly basis. This helps to gauge the take-up of the journey, from which you can set completion targets.

The simplest measure of new members is the number of visits they make in their first few weeks. The chart below shows how many new members make no visits, up to 1 visit, or more than 1 visit in their first 4 weeks. This is then compared against subsequent weekly visits. You can see that members who make no initial visits are less likely to continue, whereas most of those who make more than one weekly visit continue to do so.

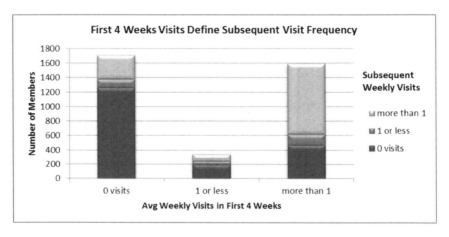

Number of new member visits in the first 4 weeks

Normalising the chart below to show the percentage of members makes the point even more clear. It demonstrates the classic Pareto principle or the 80:20 rule; if a member makes no visits in their first 4 weeks, there is an 80 per cent chance that they will not visit in subsequent weeks. Members who visit more than once in their first 4 weeks are only 20 per cent likely to make no subsequent visits.

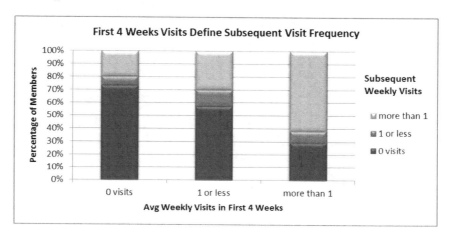

Percentage of new member visits in the first 4 weeks

It is widely known that members who don't visit much in their initial weeks are unlikely to stay with the gym, so identify these members and contact them to give some extra encouragement.

Examples of new member plans for visits in their first month

Examples of calendars showing plans for members' visits during their first month are shown below.

An adequate first month plan for a new or existing exerciser

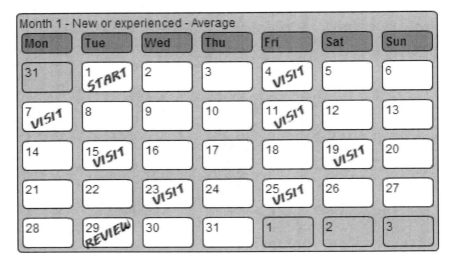

Making a couple of visits per week is the norm for a new member, or one who has exercised before. Alternatively, see if they get close to your average member's visits per week!

A reasonable first month plan for a new exerciser

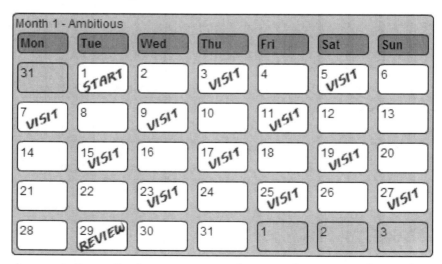

New members are likely to build up the habit slowly; one visit per week may be a big target for them, but is fine.

An over-ambitious plan for a new exerciser

Any member who is new to exercise may be setting themselves up to fail with this kind of plan, or could become burned-out and tired of the gym before they've really got into the habit.

Communicating with new members

For some budget clubs, the new member journey is focused around communication only, rather than face-to-face interactions. A welcome e-mail and/or SMS congratulate the member on joining, which is followed up by regular motivational messages throughout the new member journey time frame. These can be adapted (depending on which system you use) to send congratulatory messages to frequent visitors, and motivational messages to those who need to visit more.

Communication can be standardised for all members, but is better when adapted to individual experience and performance. Read Chapter 8 for more details. A brief introduction to new member communication which can be part of the journey is given below.

Here are some examples:

> Thanks for joining <*xyz* gym>; it's great to have you on board as a member. We look forward to seeing you again in the club very soon.

> Congratulations on visiting <*n*> times in your 1st month at <*club*>. Let us know if we can help you with anything next time you're in.

> We've not seen you down at <*club*> lately. Hope you'll be back soon... let us know how we can help you to be more motivated?

See Annex 2 for more member messaging ideas.

Summary/Actions

☐ Joining: what additional information will you collect, and how will you use it?

☐ Options: what choices (if any) does a new member have?

☐ Timescales: how long does your new member journey last?

☐ Steps: how many steps are in your new member journey; and how many of them are optional?

☐ Understand: do members and staff understand why this time frame is important?

☐ Measure: what key metrics show your journey is working, or improving retention?

3. Ongoing journey

Another big advantage of measuring the new member journey is that it has a more defined 'end', so you need to know what's next. When the new member journey just drifts off, so can your members. It benefits the member to know that there is an ongoing path that they can follow to keep them motivated and on track for their exercise goals.

The classic ongoing journey milestone is the exercise programme review, which will be explored in detail in this chapter. Other significant points are handling high-risk members, returning members, and ad-hoc member contacts.

The exercise programme review: Q & A

Why are exercise programme reviews not member focused?
Q: What is the recommended time frame for reviewing members' programmes? **A:** Every 6-8 weeks
Q: Why? **A:** To motivate members and avoid exercise plateau.
Q: Is this a good policy? **A:** No, this policy is wrong, as it does not focus on the members' needs, and is nearly always unmanageable.
Q: How is the exercise programme review unmanageable? **A:** Consider a club with 2,400 active members (visiting regularly), and 10 staff. If you review each member's programme every 8 weeks, then that is 2,400 reviews every 8 weeks, or 300 reviews per week. Each member of staff needs to do 30 programme reviews per week. On a 5-day rota, that is 6 reviews every day, for every instructor.

Q: How does it not focus on the members' needs?

A: Consider the following examples:

Greg is training for a marathon, and has a well-designed incremental programme. Two weeks after the marathon, he *wants* to set new goals and targets, so there's no need to talk to him about a programme review until then.

Becky is keen to lose weight for her wedding next summer. She does not *want* to make any changes to the programme she is currently enjoying. After 3 months, she might step-up the intensity, depending on how close to her goal she is.

Doris keeps fit in her old age, and does not *want* to add to the weight stack, or to increase the time/ distance/ intensity of her cardio exercises. She's happy to keep doing what she's doing for 6 months. If you tell Doris that she needs to change her programme in 8 weeks to stay motivated and avoid exercise plateau, you are setting her up to fail.

Programme review

Hopefully, you noticed the *wants* in the stories above. Really good exercise programmes are designed based on the member's wants, needs, and goals. Key to this is the timescale; if you ask the member when they'd like a review, and then contact them on that date, you're much more likely to deliver a quality programme review. The member feels more cared for, and will look forward to their review.

Of course, there will be a few members who don't know what they want and, for them, it is good to have a guidance timescale in mind. Base this on their experience, and always ask them if the suggested timescale sounds OK; in that way they make it their own.

If you want to read more about monitoring programme reviews due, jump to Chapter 9 (Systems).

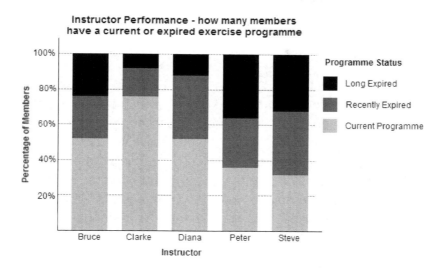

Measuring instructor performance

The programme review needs to be much more than an 'adjust the exercises, weights and timings' session. If you can help your members to set SMART goals, with particular focus on the measurable, then you will help them to get more results. Many clubs are now changing the title of the 'Programme Review' to simply a 'Review', 'Assessment' or even a 'Member Goal Review'. Read Chapter 7 (Interaction) for more on setting goals and writing a motivating exercise programme.

Case study: measuring programme review 'success'

A multi-site local authority uses Technogym's Contact Manager to record member interaction.

Shortly after implementation and training, the staff contacted over 1,200 members with expired programmes in just one month. Only about 194 members (16 per cent) actually had programme reviews, the remaining 1,019 adjusted their review date based on their wants and goals. Throughout the rest of the year, programmes were renewed and dates adjusted to be what the member wanted, rather than the standard (and unachievable) 6-8 weeks.

In the same month in the following year, there were only 412 programme reviews due, even though total membership and active members had increased; 355 programme reviews (86 per cent) were done, the remaining 67 deferred.

The instructors' schedule and focus is much improved as they know most members are ready for their review when it is due. Regardless of whether the review is done or deferred, the members' weekly visit frequency increases on average by around 50 per cent following the contact.

Consider the failure rate of programmes and effect on instructors. If every time you ask members if they want a programme review, they say 'no', then you will stop asking. If you ask them 'when' rather than 'if', and then follow-up on that date, you will have a higher success rate, and more motivated instructors and members.

High risk contact

If possible, it is really useful to be able to identify your high risk members. You can use information about how new or experienced a member is, or whether their visit frequency or exercise pattern has changed lately. Recognising and talking to members at risk is the number one priority in a lot of clubs. Make it yours too. There is more information on drop out risk (DOR) in Chapter 9 (Systems). This is not so much a step in an ongoing journey, but is a very important interaction.

Example: record interactions with high risk members only

A premium club only has one contact trigger on their system: if a member's DOR increases by more than 25 per cent in a fortnight, then contact that member. On a day-to-day basis, instructors focus on all members in the club at all times. However, if the DOR contact is triggered, it is a top priority to check the member whose risk has increased sharply, and contact them. The task is marked as done, and contact notes recorded if appropriate. This task is always effective at increasing visit frequency, and powers the club's retention strategy.

If you cannot calculate DOR at your club, but do record regular contacts, you can still trigger reminders. Just identify members for whom no contact has been recorded for 60 days, and flag to contact them again soon.

Returning members

When a member returns from a period of absence, perhaps due to injury or lack of motivation, discuss with them whether they would like to start the new journey again, or re-join the ongoing journey. By giving the member choice, you allow them to opt in to what they need; they will appreciate the steps more, and be more motivated along the way.

General contact

If you are able to record contacts in a Customer Relationship Management (CRM) or retention system, it is worth considering a 'general contact' interaction type too. This is sometimes just available as an ad-hoc exchange that can be recorded against the member records, or may be triggered when there is no recorded contact for a member in a certain time period, ensuring that all members have someone talk to them at least every <x> months.

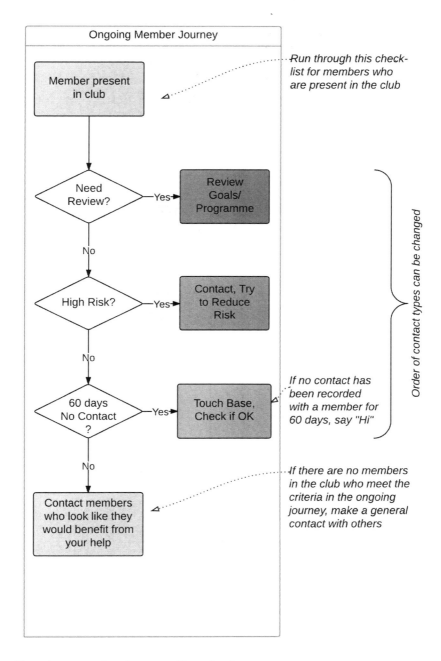

Ongoing member journey flowchart

Measure

Just as with the new member journey, it will help you to measure the ongoing journey. You will need different methods, as the number or members 'completing' the journey is not as high.

Comparing programme reviews done with programme reviews due is a good start. An example is shown below.

Monthly	Reviews Completed done	Reviews due	(%)
Bruce	25	30	83
Clarke	29	29	100
Diana	19	24	79
Peter	10	28	35
Steve	15	21	71

A comparison of reviews completed with those due

You could also compare the number of high risk visitors against the number of contacts recorded for this group, and set team (or individual) targets for them.

High Risk Visitors	High Risk Contacts	Contacted (%)
360	262	73

A comparison of high risk visitors and high risk contacts recorded

The best metric is to consider how many members are on the journey, and what proportion has slipped off track. List reasons why they could be off track, and when you have determined the number of members, work out the best way to get them back.

Recent visitors	Absentees	Active members %
1,245	1,086	53

A comparison of recent visitors, absentees and active members

Some contact management systems will show you the effectiveness of your contacts, so you know which interactions and/or staff have the best effect in keeping your members on the journey, and maximising your retention.

Summary/Actions

☐ Understanding: explain the ongoing journey to your members (all parts of it).

☐ Labels: what will you call your programme review, and what does it entail?

☐ Timescales: when would your members like a review?

☐ High Risk/Returning: how do you identify high risk and returning members?

☐ Measure: what will be your key metrics and targets?

4. Absentee 'journey'

One of the big issues in the leisure industry surrounds the creation of reports that show how good everything is, or seemingly looking through rose-tinted glasses.

For example, many clubs use the length of membership as a measurement. Unsurprisingly, an average length of membership of around 12 months is very common in clubs where 12-month contracts are popular.

A more realistic measure is the length of stay, taken from the date of the member's first visit to the last visit date. This might show that while your members pay for 12 months, they stop visiting at month 3 or 5.

Absentees are a problem at most clubs. Encourage your members to return, and they become brand advocates. If clubs focused as much time and resource on absentees as sales, then a reasonable amount of sales would come in through referrals.

This chapter looks at timescales to becoming an absentee; how to contact absentees; and who should contact them. If you never contact your absent members, they could all leave tomorrow and will undoubtedly blame the club for not helping them to achieve their goals.

The chart below shows how members could react to being contacted, or not being contacted as an absentee, and how it makes them feel after taking that action. Making contact with absent members results in positive feelings, even if the member leaves. No contact only brings negatives, which are likely be shared with friends.

	Keep Membership	Cancel Membership
Make Contact	I must go back It's my responsibility I feel positive about 'club' I'm open to more contact	I felt cared for I left feeling happy It's an ethical club I'll re-join one day I'm open to future offers
Do Nothing	I'm on a downward spiral It's getting harder to go It's been too long I feel embarrassed	I blame the club I want a refund I will never join again I'd never recommend I don't want future offers

Outcomes of making contact with absent members

Time frame

The first thing to determine is the point at which a member becomes an absentee. This could vary with membership length, as it relates to breaking the exercise habit, which is sooner for newer members. However, to keep things simple, it is best to standardise across your membership, assuming you treat new members differently.

Two weeks without a visit may be too short a timescale for members who are on holiday, whereas 5 or 6 weeks is too long; they will have broken the exercise habit, and you should have missed a member by then. If a member does not make any visits for 3-4 weeks then this is a good time to start chasing the absent member.

The diagram below shows that as the total members in each segment increases with time, the proportion of absent members grows. It is often worth looking at a sub-segment of recently absent rather than all absent, for example in members who joined more than a year ago.

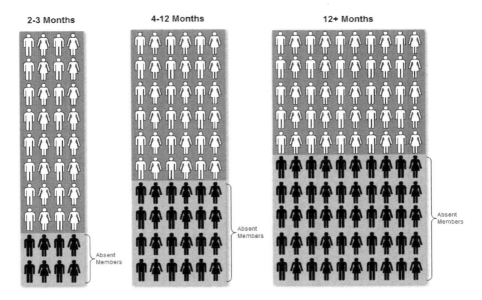

Absentee percentage grows with length of membership

How to contact absent members

There are lots of ways of communicating with individual members: a phone call, text, e-mail or a good old-fashioned letter in the post, as well as direct social media messages (if configured correctly).

The phone call is proven to be the best way of persuading members to come back into your club. However, it can be hard work and is time consuming. We'll come back to making the call, but here's how to make it easier.

Once you've decided when you're going to call the member (e.g. after 4 weeks of absence), send them a message the week before. Depending on your systems and the member's details, this could be a text, e-mail, or letter. While messages alone are less effective than calls, by adopting this approach you will increase the overall effectiveness in three ways:

1. Reduce the number of calls that need to be made

2. Warm up call (easier to make the call)

3. Make the call more effective

A few members will return because of the message, so you don't need to call them. The call is now easier to make, as you are following-up the message. And the call is now the second contact you've made, so it will have more influence on the member.

We'll come back to the script and training for making the call, but for now, know what happens next:

- If the member doesn't return, will they get another (type of) message, and then another call?

- If you left a voicemail, how soon will you try again (at another time of day)?

- How long will you keep trying to get the absent member back (forever)?

Many systems can help you to identify absent members, some will even send the messages out for you. Be sure that you change the messages regularly (we recommend doing so every month) to keep them personalised, and link them to your club promotions and events. You should also monitor and measure the success rates of messages and calls.

Some budget clubs and local authorities just send messages to absent members, as they don't have the resources to make the calls. The process is the same, but different rules apply, and it can still persuade members to return.

Call your absent members to coax them back, but also use the other contact details they gave you to increase the chance of keeping them as members.

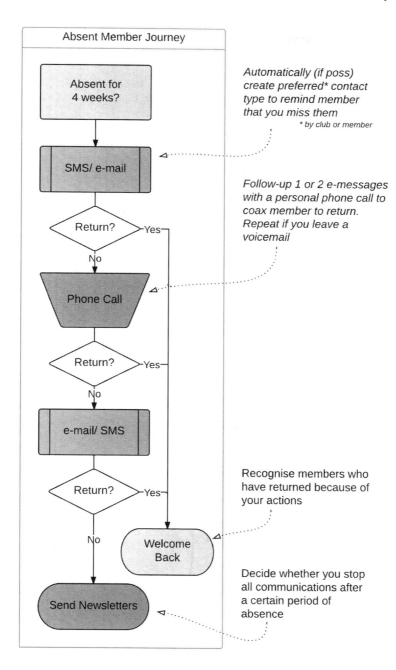

Absent member journey flowchart

Who's going to make the call?

Calling absent members is one of the least popular jobs in the gym. Most instructors prefer cleaning to calling absentees. Sure, the gym needs to be clean, otherwise people will leave, but you could stop six people from dropping out by spending 30 minutes on a few phone calls.

The gym team are usually the ideal staff to call absent members and encourage them back into the club. They should have the best relationship with the members, having talked about their needs, goals, habits and exercise programme. Alternatively, you might have the person who signed up the member in the first place (useful for new absentees), or a retention officer or membership manager who makes all the calls. The best person to make the calls in your club is the one who is most likely to actually make the calls!

You could stop six people from dropping out by spending 30 minutes on a few phone calls

It's important that the team know why *they* are making the calls, and what it is they are trying to achieve. If you need another carrot and stick to help instructors to make the calls, then:

• Provide training and support in making the calls (carrot)

• Include calling absentees in the team's job description (stick)

A call is successful when the member returns to the club, not when they promise to do so, or when a voicemail message has been left. Knowing what outcomes are acceptable and what follows is a key part of the process. If the member does not return after having received a call, when do you call again? How long after leaving a voice message do you try again? It can help staff to know that they have to record, say, three attempts before the contact is passed onto the membership manager; this way it is not an endless task.

So we now know that the intended outcome is to get the member back into the club. In retention workshops we have found that instructors don't like 'cold calling', and don't know what to say to absent members. Role play is about as popular as making phone calls, but it can help with these issues...

Members do not join a club intending to leave. Good fitness instructors are motivated by helping people to get fitter or achieving their fitness goals. If you are selling anything, it is health and fitness, but it is certainly not cold calling!

Knowing what to say is simple if you have a little information from the front of house or retention system. As well as their name and phone number, know when each member joined and last visited as a minimum. Bonus information might be their fitness goals and visit history, along with other recorded attempts to get them back. If a message has already been sent, this is a great ice-breaker; for example, 'I'm just following up the message we sent last week...'

Contacting absent members should just be another regular task in the running of a successful club. It is part of good customer service, or trying to deliver health and fitness to your members. Some of them need extra help, and will really appreciate your efforts.

Summary/Actions

☐ How long before a member becomes 'absent'?

☐ How will you contact them in the first instance with a reminder? Will you start with a text, a call, or other methods?

☐ If you call your absent members, who will make the calls, and will they be recorded?

☐ How many times will you call members?

☐ What happens next... do you cancel or suspend their membership?

5. Ex-members

The final part of your member journey should describe what happens to members as they leave. Too often, members leave feeling dissatisfied, and the leaving process of many clubs adds to this feeling. The worst clubs are those which delete members' details as soon as they leave.

Are there alternatives?

If a member wants to leave, the very first thing you need to do is find out why. Next, you can find out if there is anything you can do to help them stick around. Sometimes it will be too late, but a membership suspension, discount, or other offer might turn them around.

Impossible situations and ideas to reverse them

Member:	'I want to leave; I can't afford the gym anymore.'
Staff:	'Can you refer any friends? You get a monthly referral commission; if you get 5 friends to join, it would halve your monthly fees.'
Member:	'I want to leave, I'm not getting any closer to my goals.'
Staff:	'If you stay for another 3 months, I could get the club to pay for 3 PT sessions to help your motivation.'
Member:	'I want to leave. I'm injured and can't train for a while.'
Staff:	'If you don't want to do any other exercise, I could suspend your membership and reduce your monthly payments to a nominal £<xx>, which will make it easier (cheaper) to get started again once you're better.'

Make it easy

Contracts and collections aside, you need to make the leaving process relatively easy and simple. Sometimes you need to impose the contract terms and conditions, and collect the dues, but by making the process easy you have more chance of getting the member back in the future.

Information is key

As the member leaves, you must record the reason and ask for feedback about your club. This could form part of the online leaving process, or be made through an exit interview or call. You must be interested in this information, particularly if it presents a challenge that you can address and stop others following this member. Just by looking interested and perhaps even saying 'sorry' (which costs nothing), it leaves the door open, and gives a vital opportunity to check the member's contact details.

Example leave form

Application to Suspend/Cancel membership

Your Name: _____

E-mail: _____

Membership: _____

Reason: ☐ Health ☐ Lack of results ☐ Cost
☐ Moving ☐ Dissatisfied
☐ Other _____ (please specify)

Please: ☐ Could I suspend until _____?
☐ Could I cancel my membership?

Please rate our:	Excellent	Good	Average	Poor
Staff support:	☐	☐	☐	☐
Equipment:	☐	☐	☐	☐
Cleanliness:	☐	☐	☐	☐
Value for money:	☐	☐	☐	☐

Are you:
☐ joining another club
☐ already a member at another club
☐ exercising outside / at home
☐ having a rest from exercise?

Office use only:

Join Date: _____ Leave Date: _____ LoM: _____

Subsequent contact

Around a month later, you should ask again why the member left (referring to the last reason given if possible). Again this could be made during a call, or via an online survey, for example. It is surprising how different an ex-member's answers can be from those originally given, after having had time to 'cool off'. You get the chance to find out if they've joined another club, and to say that your door is still open to them.

Thereafter, all ex-members should be contacted regularly (we suggest quarterly) with a newsletter, survey, offers and promotions; for example, an extension of the standard open weekend to include Friday and Monday for ex-members... something to get them back into the club.

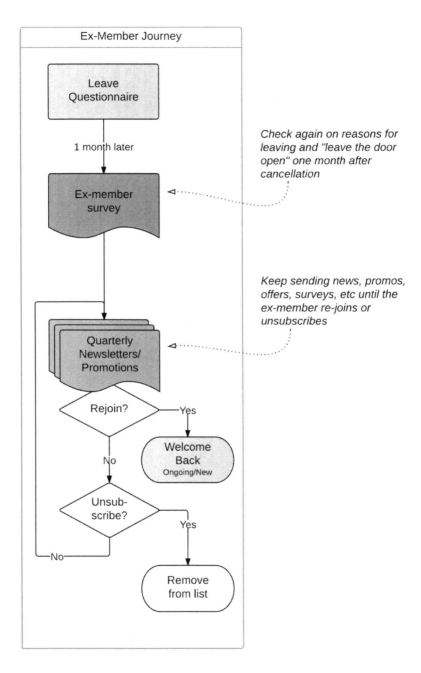

Ex-member journey flowchart

Summary/Actions

☐ Before a member leaves, find out why they want to leave and offer alternatives.

☐ Make the leaving process as easy as possible, but...

☐ Get as much valuable information from leavers as possible.

☐ Follow-up a month later, and then at regular intervals.

PART 2

People

Interaction and
Communication

Systems

6. People

People are the best component in an effective member-retention policy. A club with the most sophisticated systems, state-of-the-art equipment, and excellent location may have good retention, but it can always be bettered by introducing good staff. Conversely, a club with brilliant, motivated staff can have very good member retention rates, regardless of systems, kit or location.

To build and maintain a brilliant, motivated team, you need to ensure your staff have purpose, good leadership, understanding, and buy-in. The journey and communication processes in this book help define standards and provide guidelines for your team, but motivation comes from a deeper place.

Some budget clubs work with a minimal staff model and less focus on people. They use communication and systems analysis to affect retention, and we are learning a lot about members' behaviour and trends from this data. There are clever people working behind the scenes on member data, but the best effect is found when there are good people front of house as well.

Purpose

Why are you here? This is often the opening question at the start of a retention workshop. You might ask yourself why you are reading this book.

Finding what motivates people is key to understanding them and to helping them to understand themselves. If you are going to be successful and happy, you need to know your purpose, or what drives you as a person.

In the fitness industry, few people are driven by making lots of money (if they are, they are unlikely to be satisfied). Most staff, particularly fitness instructors and management are inspired by helping people to get healthier and fitter, or to quote the ukactive (formerly the Fitness Industry Association) mantra, 'get more people, more active, more often'.

Compare the activities undertaken by Adam and Zac during their shifts.

Shifts: Adam and Zak

Adam	Zak
Open Gym	Open Gym
3 x Programme Reviews	Cleaning
Phone 5 absent members	Talk to PTs about qualifications
Speak to high risk members	Speak to free weight users
Contact tomorrow's appts	Moan about program no-shows
Ad-hoc programme tweaks	Leave notice on out of order kit
Log broken kit with service co.	

It is clear which instructor is having a better effect on member retention, and who is working harder, but consider also who is having a better day. Who goes home feeling fulfilled and looking forward to tomorrow? Cleaning and equipment maintenance needs to be done to keep the club open, but it is not what keeps members returning to the club.

There are some instructors and staff in the fitness industry who have lost their purpose, or never really had it in the first place. They are happy to do the chores like cleaning before working on any purposeful task such as phoning or speaking to members. Perhaps they just enjoy an easy life watching people in a gym. It is the purpose of this book, and one of our goals to help these staff to realise their purpose, or to move on.

Staff goals

It's helpful to discuss your staff's work and life goals, to know what they are working towards, and to help and support them in their journey. As well as individual goals, agreed team goals help to create a good team culture and engender purpose in your staff.

Setting exercise goals is one of the fundamental parts of the Chapter 7 (Interaction) and, as such, it is important that staff do the same. It's not only good to practice goal setting, but good for the team if everyone sets and shares their individual exercise goals. It helps people understand each other, making the team bond stronger, and staff can play to their strengths and recommend each other to members for programme reviews and exercise tips.

Gym manager

Too often, the gym manager is the longest serving instructor, has the most members, and opens and/or closes the gym most days.

Leading by example is all very well, but a successful gym manager needs to look after only a few members (or even none), but focus on inspiring and motivating staff to keep their members motivated. As well as focusing on their staff, the gym manager also needs to communicate with other departments and management on team performance.

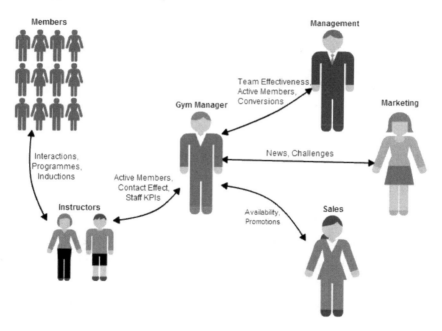

Gym manager as hub - Staff interaction routes in the club

Examples of feedback from the gym manager

> **To Staff:**
>
> ☐ number of members*   ☐ number of active members
>
> ☐ contact effectiveness   ☐ reviews done/due
>
> * some managers get instructors to report this to them
>
>
> **To Management:**
>
> ☐ team effectiveness   ☐ active members (%)
>
> ☐ high DOR contacts (%)   ☐ inductions complete
>
> ☐ challenges taken up / completed

Understanding and buy-in

All staff need to have a good understanding of the system or processes that are in place, and how they help members and staff. A good test is if an instructor can explain to a member why they contact them at a certain point in the journey, or what the benefits are to joining a certain challenge. Someone who 'sells' the process really well demonstrates that they buy-in to the ideas.

Communications are critical, not just from staff to members, but internally. Provide regular feedback on performance and targets. Brainstorm on what is working well, and what could be adapted. This will help with buy-in and reinforce the system and purpose.

On show

Last, but not least, appearance and approachability of staff is vital. You are always on show. The most successful clubs are those which really go to town on dress code and protocol. Try a few of these gym rules for size; perhaps have a top five rules or customer charter for your club:

- Always be approachable

- Members come first, before discussions with other staff

- Smile and say 'Hello' to everyone within 5 metres

- No team huddles when on duty
  (spread out and look approachable)

- Never leave the gym floor unattended

- Use first names wherever possible (learn them)

- No extended chatting (staff, and members?)

Some other basic rules include:

- No litter, gym floor always clean and tidy

- Uniform always clean, neat, name badge clearly visible

- Don't ever look bored; there's always something to do

- Take your break outside of the gym

- No reading on duty

- No mobiles on duty

- No eating on duty

Personal trainers

How do personal trainers (PTs) help to deliver great member retention, and what can clubs and staff learn from them?

Many gym staff aspire to be personal trainers. Some are motivated by the 'money', but instructors who make the transition successfully are likely to be focused on interaction and getting results.

Good PTs have great client retention and are therefore a big asset to a club. Their retention is good because they have to interact with all their clients regularly, and they know their customers really well.

The client arrives for an appointment knowing what to expect, and leaves with another appointment booked. They will hopefully visit again or do some form of exercise before the next PT session, but there is a milestone in the calendar, and it is always clear where they are in the journey.

Qualifications, drive and sound business sense are important prerequisites if you want to become a PT. But brilliant interaction skills will help you to get results for your members, which is the magic wand that you need. This is also what the best clubs (those which care about retaining members) are looking for in their staff.

Personal trainers need to comply with other staff on systems, procedures, communications, and so on. In other words, they ideally need to integrate with the club to truly help with retention.

At some budget clubs, PTs are the only staff, and they deliver inductions for new members as part of their rent agreement. If you have great, interactive PTs, this will help retention and also helps the PT to get more business. You never know where a lead will come from, and offering free advice is a much better way to sell the services of a PT.

Summary/Actions

☐ Great people are the key to great retention.

☐ Ensure you and your staff have purpose.

☐ Understand and buy-in to the systems and processes.

☐ Always strive to improve internal communication.

☐ Wear the uniform with pride.

7. Interaction

Many fitness professionals come out of college with a wealth of exercise and fitness knowledge, but needing more confidence in terms of their interpersonal skills. Confidence builds with time and practice, but this chapter will hopefully make that practice easier and provide a fast-track to more confidence and more effective interaction, more often.

Say 'Hello'

It might sound simple, but greeting people with 'Hello' is a great place to start. Say 'Hello' or 'Hi' to every member that comes through the door, or that you come into contact with. This is a great icebreaker and will make you more approachable. It also helps to break down any internal barriers you might have to interacting more with members.

There comes a point where you've said 'Hello' to the same member every day for a week, and you need to say something more. There are more ideas below, but a good next step is to tell the member your name, and offer to help. At least half will tell you their name in return; and you can just ask the remainder for their name. Most will turn down the offer of help, but saying 'just ask when you do' leaves it open, and breaks the ice even more.

Instructors find it useful is to have a selection of interaction types to choose from. Here are some examples:

- Induction/First Appointment/Welcome

- Check-up/Review/Second/Third Appointment

- Programme Review

- High Risk Contact

- Absentee Return

- General/Ad-hoc Contact

Classifying contact types makes it easier for instructors to interact with members. If you have a system to record or trigger contact reminders, then a few contact types are really helpful. You may even be able to show the effect of different contact types on members' visit patterns, and focus on certain contacts or set targets.

Start with the end in mind

Before you set out to talk to a member, think about what you are trying to achieve. You might be trying to find out about the member, to check if their exercise programme is still suitable, how they are progressing towards their goal, or simply finding out their name. Ultimately, if you are doing something to engage the member more and motivate them to visit as regularly or more regularly, then everyone's winning.

A successful interaction

Beyond the greeting, or finding out a member's name, a successful interaction can be broken down into three components.

Introduction

The introduction should start before you approach the member. Find out about them if you can: their exercise aspirations or goals, programme status, visit history or length of membership. A couple of facts will do, along with their name, and then check on what it is you are trying to achieve with the contact.

Of course it may be that the member approaches you, in which case you may not have time for research. If you don't know it, finding out their name is essential, so tell them your name (even if you're wearing a badge) as most will reply with theirs. Find out more by moving straight into open questions with something like 'How can I help?'

Open questions and listening

Now you're chatting to the member, you need to find out more about their exercise habits, or attend to their needs. If you ask open questions (ones that cannot be answered with a simple 'yes' or 'no'), it helps the member to explain what they need and gives you the chance to listen to them. Once you have really listened and understood what the member wants, you can move on to discuss how they are going to get it.

Actions (follow-up)

To round off the contact, it's best to summarise the actions and time frames. If there are pledges here, it is best that they are the member's promises, rather than the instructor's. The member should set the actions and timescale to follow-up, as they are then much more likely to take responsibility.

Examples of open and closed questions

There's a reason we have two ears and only one mouth: it is often better to listen than to speak, particularly when you are part of delivering a great service. If you take the time to really understand what the customer wants, then you can help them to get it. Closed questions can be a good place to start, as they are quick and easy to answer, but open questions reveal more, make the respondent think, and give you an insight into their feelings. Open questions also help with the listening process. Here are a few examples of open and closed questions:

Closed	Open
Are you enjoying your workout?	What do you enjoy about your workout?
Will you reach your goal?	How are you going to reach your goal?
Would you like to visit the gym more?	Why would you like to visit the gym more?
Does that work for you?	Describe how that feels to you?

Closed questions often begin with words like *are, do, will, would,* and elicit one-word answers, or a yes/no. Open questions use words like *how, what, why, describe,* and get the member to open up and tell you more.

Goal setting

Goals are really important for member retention. If you have a decent goal, it's much easier to monitor progression. And if your members can clearly see what they are achieving, they are much more likely to stick around, as shown in the diagram below.

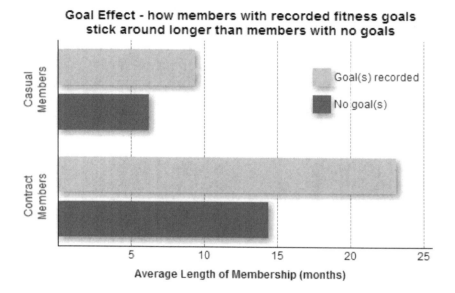

The effects of goal setting on gym membership

But what is a decent goal? It is said that 80 per cent of gym members join to lose weight. Others want to maintain or improve fitness or strength. These goals lack definition though, so it is important to understand how to describe your goals, and to record and share them.

The most common mnemonic used in goal setting is SMART, which has a variety of associations, but for our purposes, the most common ones are:

S	**Specific**
M	**Measurable**
A	**Attainable**
R	**Responsible**
T	**Timely**

When recording a goal, you don't need to use a bullet point for each of the five parts, but you should check that all points are covered. We'll come back onto goal sharing in a moment, but the other key part is writing the goal down. The person setting the goal (the member, not the instructor) should write down their goal, as this helps them to visualise and take responsibility for the goal. Of course, if the instructor also records the goal, that's great for ongoing support.

A good exercise for instructors is to rewrite some standard goals as a SMART goal.

Here are a few examples of SMART goals that groups of fitness professionals came up with at a retention workshop, using role play and working with each other as members. They include SMART goals that relate to losing weight, keeping fit and gaining strength.

SMART Goals - Losing weight

☐ It is 14 February and I can fit into my size 12 dresses.

☐ It is the end of January and I can walk all the way up the escalator at Tottenham Court Road without being out of breath.

☐ I feel good on the beach in my bikini on my holiday in March.

☐ I have more choice when shopping for clothes in the January sales.

☐ It's the end of December and I have visited the gym at least once a week.

Often the most difficult type of member to set goals with is one who doesn't want or need to lose weight, but joins the gym to keep fit. The good news is that these members usually have good motivation already, but it's still important to help them to set some SMART goals to keep their motivation levels up in times of trouble.

SMART Goals - Keeping fit

☐ I will complete my charity 10km run in April in under 45 minutes.

☐ By 31st May I can swim 15 lengths of the pool non stop.

☐ I've been skiing for a week in January and am not completely knackered at the end of each day.

☐ I can play a full game of 5-a-side without needing a sub break by March.

☐ I've completed the London to Brighton bike ride (June).

The third type of member on our course was the person who wanted to gain strength. Now most fitness professionals love these members; they often identify with them and want to jump straight onto the bench press or smith machine and pump some iron. However, to monitor progress and maintain motivation, it's still important to set SMART goals.

SMART Goals - Gaining strength

☐ It's now *<date>* and I can bench press 3 ×10 sets of *<x>* kg and squat 3 ×10 sets of *<x>* kg.

☐ My biceps / thighs measure *<x>* cm by April.

☐ I'm stronger, so I am able to make more tackles and shake off more tacklers when playing rugby in February.

☐ I am competing in Mr/Mrs Universe next summer.

☐ I can hit the golf/tennis ball further/harder at the start of next season.

Not all the above goals cover all the bases of SMART, but they are good varied examples. You might check with the individual member on whether the goal is attainable and if they take responsibility for the goal.

These examples are given to help SMART goal setting, not to be assigned to your members. Remember that a goal is personal and, as such, all members' goals should be different. You can help them to measure progress, and keep their motivation going by helping them to move towards the goal.

Responsibility

Once your member has set their SMART goal(s), it's important to check their commitment and motivation to reach the goal, and to ensure that they take responsibility for achieving it.

Discussing how they will feel when they have reached the goal is important in order to assess their motivation levels. It may also be worth talking through what they will lose as a result of achieving their goal, and ensuring the balance is still positive.

Finding out what could delay or get in the way of the end goal is another good way of checking commitment. If the member knows how they will manage these set-backs, it helps them to focus on the goal and adds motivation.

Finally, it's imperative that the member takes responsibility for the goal. Sure, you're going to help them along the way, but responsibility lies with them. If they have the option to blame you or someone else for not reaching the goal, then they are not fully committed, and you should go back over the previous steps with the member.

Challenges

Member challenges are a great way to add a little extra motivation or drive to members in your club. If they can be aligned with members' goals too, they will appeal even more.

It is best to keep the challenges simple, but varied. An Olympic decathlon of exercises will probably be too much for all but the very keen member (who is unlikely to leave anyway), but a triathlon of rowing machine, upright bike, treadmill, will appeal to more members.

Simple challenge examples	
Visits	The most, or everyone who exceeds 12 visits in one month wins…
Distance	Furthest travelled, or everyone who travels <x> km wins…
Calories	The member who burns most wins…
Moves	The member who records the greatest number of moves. Members' pedometers can record moves inside and outside the club

Think through the challenges before you start: who are you trying to appeal to, how will it improve retention, and does it include all, or exclude certain members? Will you run concurrent challenges, or one at a time? Announcing the next challenge early gives members time to prepare (or prepare an excuse!).

Challenges are great for new members; usually based on visits to the club to help your new members to get into the exercise habit. Prizes can include a t-shirt, guest passes, or class vouchers, whatever your members will value (perhaps you could let them choose).

Prizes should of course be relevant to the challenge, and a lot of members will be happy that they've been more motivated to achieve their goal, without receiving a token prize. If you have a challenge that does really deliver more visits and more motivated members, then the additional income should easily cover something more meaningful for your members.

Bespoke challenges could be set for new members, or existing members who have had a goal review, or they could help to generate a new individual challenge or join a team challenge.

Team challenges

Most gym challenges are for individuals, but team challenges can really help motivation, particularly if the teams are led by instructors. This gets your instructors to 'sell' the challenge to your members, and encourage them to help the team to win. It can generate small clubs within clubs, communities competing with each other to help their team leader to be 'top dog'.

If you have instructors on board with challenges, it makes them much more engaging for members. Regular updates on the leader-board will help to motivate participants and generate more interaction around your club.

Involve a local charity, or join in regular charity events to take challenges outside your club, and provide all participants with branded club t-shirts to show they are part of the team. This also gives members a sponsorship incentive to help achieve their goals.

More challenge ideas can be found in Appendix 2.

Classes

There is no doubt that classes are a big part of some clubs' retention strategy, and members either love classes or don't bother with them. Getting members to exercise in groups does have a positive effect on retention; in fact, some very successful fitness businesses are built solely on group exercise, without fixed locations or buildings.

One of the reasons why classes help to retain members is the interaction that they provide for members, both with the instructor, and with other class members. It is important to foster this process, to try and ensure everyone is involved or has some interaction, even if it is just a 'hello' or 'goodbye' at the beginning or end of the class.

Encouraging members to join classes is good way to boost retention, particularly if you can convert class-phobic members into promoters.

Encourage members to join classes

Getting new members into classes should always be encouraged. Here are a few ideas.

- Give new members a free pass when they join.

- Offer regular taster sessions– 10-minute introductions.

- Announce availability of spaces in a class to everyone present in the club.

- Give a member a bonus free class if they bring a friend.

Summary/Actions

☐ 'Hello' is the simplest, but often most effective interaction; use it as much as you can.

☐ Know the three stages of a successful interaction:

    1. Introduction (including research)

    2. Open questioning and listening

    3. Actions (and responsibility)

☐ Set goals with your members; ensure that they take responsibility.

☐ Work with your members to help them achieve their goals.

☐ Set-up challenges to increase member motivation.

☐ Involve more members in classes, and interact with everyone in the class.

8. Communication

We live in an age where communication has become extremely low cost, and it is easy to send an e-mail to hundreds or thousands of members, or to text prospects. This makes meaningful face-to-face contact more valuable, which is why the information given in the last two chapters on people and interaction is so important to many clubs.

However, there is a place for bulk communications in member retention, whether it is a monthly newsletter, new member tips, or absentee reminders. Budget clubs with a low-staff model use automatic communication to good effect. Good member segmentation and personalising the message are key to the success of member retention messages.

Segmentation

Dividing your members into different segments allows you to focus or target your communications. It can also save costs. Too many segments can make things complicated though, and you may spend more time and resources than you would have saved, to no great gain. Keeping it simple is always best. Here are some examples of segments.

Experience   **Goals**

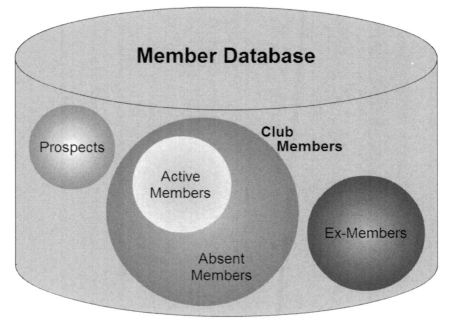

Membership status/visit segmentation

The diagram below illustrates how absent members can be split into further segments to control and monitor communication to give you the best chance to get absent members to return. After 3 weeks of not visiting the gym, members are considered to be absent, but after 7 weeks, they flow into a recovery pool, which itself can flow into a dormant pool 14 weeks later.

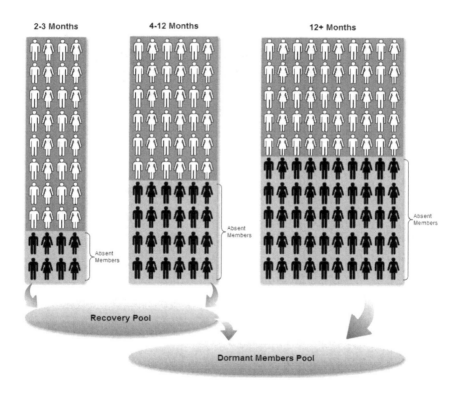

Absentees and flow into recovery and dormant segments

You could also consider segmenting by contract type, age group, gender, or whether a member has shown an interest (or ever attended) a group exercise class.

Any segmentation should have a purpose; that is, you will treat people differently, send them a tailored communication, or exclude them from certain communications, depending on their segments.

Communication channels

Deciding what communication channels are available comes next; traditional methods are post, e-mail and text. Within each channel, there may be different options; for example you could post a renewal letter, certificate of achievement, promotional postcard, or birthday card. E-mail is good for reaching all your members (or just active members?) with a monthly newsletter, or for personalised reminders about new classes, for example. An SMS text message is great for sending a reminder about a class booking, or to chase absentees.

There are pros and cons for all the different methods of communication. E-mail is great for bulk messaging, but open rates in the health and fitness industry are only around 20 per cent, with around 5 per cent of recipients clicking on a link. If you send 1,000 e-mails, you could expect about 50 clicks on one of the links therein. Although it is more likely that 1,000 letters will be opened, it's more difficult to get people onto the web from a letter, so you might just be trying to get them back into the club with news of a not-to-be-missed event, or offer. SMS texts are often read instantly but need to be short and to the point.

Pros and cons of different communication methods

Method	Pros	Cons
Face-to-face	Best, guaranteed	Only members in club
Phone call	Good for absentees	Resource intensive
SMS msg	Prompt for absentees	Limited text
E-mail	Cheap, include links	Impersonal, ignored?
Postcard	Nice to receive	Relatively expensive
Letter	Personal, shows value	Expensive
Social media	Cheap, wide reaching	Hard to collate details

Social Media

Social media messaging is a relatively new channel that is currently being used very effectively by clubs for marketing and generic retention messages. While it is possible to send direct communications to members via social networks, until we collect members' Twitter or Facebook details at sign-up, it is better to focus and measure the traditional communication methods of letter, e-mail and SMS messaging.

Some communication methods used for different members

	New	Existing (regular)	Existing (reminder)	Absent	Ex-
Face-to-face	Y	Y			
Phone call	Y		Y	Y	
SMS msg	Y		Y	Y	Y
E-mail	Y	Y		Y	Y
Postcard				Y	
Letter	Y			Y	Y
Social media		Y	Y		

Manual messages

Before considering automating messages to your members, first think about when you would usually send messages manually and who would send them. A personal ad-hoc message to a member from an instructor is normally highly appreciated. However, you might want to provide templates for your staff so that they stay on message, or within corporate guidelines.

Personalisation

You improve the effectiveness of your messages by personalising them. Using the member's first name in the greeting line should be standard, and incorporating any other personal detail can also make the message look more 'hand-written'. For example, use information about the member's visit history, join date, next review date, or goal progress.

Opt-in

Electronic marketing rules are there to protect members' privacy, so you should respect their wishes and ask them to opt-in to receiving electronic communications. However, if you have only one 'receive info' tick box, and the member opts-out, then you've shut off all communication channels.

It is better to flag an opt-in for each channel you use: post, e-mail, SMS, and so on. If a member chooses to opt-out of one, you still have other means of communication available. Sell the communication options to members as well; you are not going to pass their details onto an insurance company; they will be used by the club and instructors to keep motivating the member to get results!

Another interesting method used by a small number of clubs is to not ask members to opt-in in when taking the member or prospect's details, but send an e-mail and/or text shortly afterwards, which of course includes all the necessary opt-out details. It is advisable (a legal obligation) to get members' consent before sending them electronic communications (the permission to send messages may be granted in the small print of the sign-up form); but those clubs that use this method do maintain good opt-in rates. Making the first couple of communications compelling is key to keeping members engaged.

New members

A welcome message is not just a nice thing to do for new members; it also opens up the communication channels, and establishes the permission to contact the member throughout the journey of their membership. It should be personalised somehow, and talk about helping the member to build up the exercise habit, with a mutual commitment to help them achieve their desired results.

There could also be a message of congratulation to members who 'graduate' through the new member journey. Any new member who has visited regularly for the first x weeks receives a reminder that they're now due a review, or to touch base to see if they need any more guidance.

New members who aren't visiting as much need more attention, particularly if you can't speak to them in the club. This is a critical time; and sending a weekly text or e-mail to new members who haven't visited can really help retention, in both the long and short term. Members need to build up the habit of attending the gym and, whether they are on contract or not, if they're not visiting in the initial weeks, then you will struggle to retain them.

The flowchart below is an example of a new member communication journey, showing where interactions happen, triggered by the visit level of members after they join.

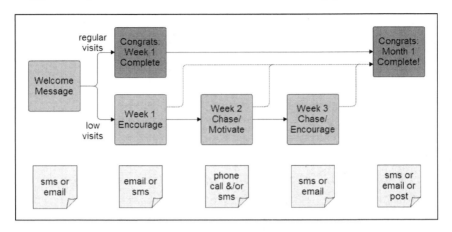

Communication journey: new member

Newsletters

A regular newsletter is a good way to stay in touch with all members who are not considered to be new, high risk, absent, and so on; in other words, your regular members.

The key to keeping newsletters fresh is to have:

1. Good content

2. A hook to make members look forward to opening

3. Not too much information

Surveys can also help to engage members, particularly if you publish and act on their results (see below).

If you can plan ahead with your news content, including stories, competitions, and offers, then it is easy to get a regular newsletter out that your members look forward to receiving.

The newsletter content can also be used in ex-member or prospect mailings, along with relevant offers (see below for more information).

Surveys

A great way to engage fully with your existing members and keep them coming back for more is to run regular member surveys. Look forward a couple of pages for information about ex-member surveys.

Many clubs see surveys as a chore: the standard SERVQUAL questionnaires are printed out and 100 members are badgered to answer the questions. However, if you make a member survey easy, quick, and interesting to answer, it will reap retention rewards.

Three steps to a successful survey

1. Do the survey (you'll find tips and tools below).

2. Publish the results to all members. This shows your members what their views are as a group, and where their opinions fit in the club.

3. Act on the results. Your members will see that you have taken note of what they think, and you will get more responses next time around.

When it comes to the questions, first think what you want to find out, and define the questions accordingly. To make results analysis easy, define the answers as well: yes/no /don't know; or a sliding scale of poor to excellent; or a scale of 1 to 5.

Comments or free format fields can add valuable feedback or elaboration on the answers. We recommend asking no more than three questions. Explain at the start why you value the member's opinion and that the three questions will take only one minute, and you will receive many more responses.

Clubs with the Technogym Wellness System have a fantastic survey tool, which can offer questionnaires to members as they check into the gym. Member segmentation, opt-out and results graphs are all key features. Survey Monkey is the leading online survey tool that you can embed into your newsletters, websites or social media sites. And if you want to keep it really simple, Facebook has 'Questions', or you could just ask your followers on Twitter what they think about certain issues.

Get your staff involved by asking them to complete the survey before it goes live. This ensures that all questions and answers are clear. It also enables staff to talk to members about the survey and encourage more responses. Ensure that staff are aware of the outcome once the survey closes. It is much easier to understand results when they are displayed as graphs or pictures, and many tools do this automatically if the survey is built right.

Remember to keep your surveys simple and regular. Carry out the survey, publish the results, and act on them. Make changes based on what your members want, not what you think they want.

There is more information about surveys and examples in Appendix 2.

Absentees

There will always be a few members who are visiting less, or not at all. Early identification is crucial, and sending a message (text or e-mail) is a great way to start to re-engage them. The message will encourage a few absentees back, reducing the number of calls that need to be made. It also gives whoever is making the calls a good opening gambit; for example, 'Did you receive the e-mail/text we sent last week? I'm just following up to see what we can do to help you get back down to the club.'

Timing is everything for absentee messages, from when they are sent, to how many messages are sent to each member, and for how long. Systems are available that provide automated messaging to contact absent members with pre-defined or tailored messages.

There is often debate as to how long you should continue to contact absent members. Many clubs will let the sleeping dogs lie, whereas super-ethical clubs will contact absent members until they return, or cancel. There is something to be said for contacting all your absent members; if you do encourage them to leave, then when they look to re-join a club, yours will be top of the list.

The flowchart below is an example of a communications journey for an absent member, combining different communication methods, and an option to follow-up in different ways depending on the outcome of the 5 week call.

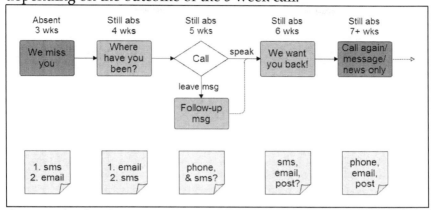

Communication journey: absent member

Ex-members

Communication with ex-members was mentioned in Chapter 5, but it's worth re-capping here.

How to generate £3,000 by sending an e-mail

A budget gym chain sent an e-mail survey newsletter to 6,000 ex-members who had left in the previous 12 months. Each person who completed the survey received the option to re-join for 6 months for the price of 3.

The survey questions were simple, but the results were not important. The first question asked why they joined in the first place (value, location, contract, staff, equipment, etc.); another used the net promoter question, 'On a scale of 1-10 would you recommend the club to a friend?'. There were just four questions in total; while the results were analysed, the main purpose was not to poll ex-members views, but to get them to rejoin, or just stay in touch.

There were around 100 negative or abusive responses, which were put to one side and followed-up (or ignored/unsubscribed) later.

Around 200 members completed the survey, and 32 used the offer code generated. This created at least £1,440 in revenue, but returning members at this chain typically stay for 10 months, so the projected revenue (with 3 months free) is £3,360. Other ex-members may have joined as a result of the survey, but this was not tracked.

Ex-member surveys are now sent quarterly, with slightly differing questions, with and without re-joining offers.

Measure

Measuring and adapting written communications is easy enough with e-mail and text. Deliveries and opens, rejects and unsubscribes are standard metrics that show you how engaged members are, and click-through rates on links show how appealing your content is. It is more difficult to measure the effectiveness of letters, but sometimes enclosing a simple voucher, or asking 'Did you get/like the letter?' is a good way of recording the impact of the message.

Summary/Actions

☐ Communication needs to be regular and appropriate.

☐ Send new members weekly tips, and open communication channels with them in the early stages of their membership.

☐ Ensure that members who attend regularly receive regular newsletters to keep them abreast of club developments, offers and events.

☐ Contact absent members and try to encourage them to return.

9. Systems

Retention systems can cost just a few pounds or thousands of pounds. Similar results can be achieved with various systems regardless of price; the success of any system is related to the people and processes involved.

Some systems can become so complex that they confuse everyone who uses them, and despite all the modules and promises of more engaged members, the technical (i.e. computer) retention system often falls into disuse.

When implementing any (technical or non-technical) system, it is paramount to keep it simple, or KISS (Keep It Simple, Stupid). Be absolutely clear on the process and the purpose of each stage. If part of the process becomes too complex to explain to staff, then you should break it down into smaller parts, or stage the implementation of the ideas.

Simple retention systems

One of the cheapest and simplest retention systems is the member card file. Every member has a coloured A5 card, which is filed alphabetically in a box in the club reception, and members record their attendance each time they visit. In some cases, the exercise programme is also recorded on the card.

Key to this system is the process. A member of staff regularly (weekly or fortnightly) goes through the whole card file, and removes the cards for all members who have not visited for a certain period (say, 4 weeks). These cards are filed in a different, 'absent members' box. When an absent member returns, they request their card is taken from the absent box, and are welcomed back, or given special attention.

As members cards are removed to the absent box, members are also sent a message to encourage them to return (see Chapter 8, Communication). If you want to make the system more complex, you could contact all members whose cards are in the absent box. Or to reduce message costs, move cards from the absent box after another 4 weeks to another 'long absent' box, and only send those members the occasional special offer.

Exercise Card File - a simple retention system

Variations on the same theme can add complexity, but increase effectiveness if executed well.

For a 'workout factory', members can clock-in with the card so that it is time-stamped. Clock-out times also might add value (more about this later when we look at technical systems).

Sticky notes can be attached to cards for rewards or competitions (e.g. more than 10 workouts in a month), which can be redeemed for awards. Sticky notes are also used for flagging details of those members whose exercise programme has expired.

Different coloured cards can be used, which are changed every quarter to show members who are visiting infrequently, but have not had a programme review for some time. For example, start the year with green member cards, change to red in Q2 as members visit and move onto a new programme, and by the time you change to yellow in Q3, members who are still on green cards will be clearly detected.

Coloured wristbands may also appeal to members; at their discretion, they can choose to wear a new member's wristband for the first few weeks, or a colour relating to their programme status, a principle that is much like the coloured card system above.

This system and variations work well at many small gyms, but it does not always scale well. When there are somewhere between 500 and 1,000 members, staffing time or costs can become unmanageable or prohibitive, unless you have a lot of cheap staff resources (such as free memberships).

Computer based system

The other end of the scale in terms of managing retention is a computer based system. A computer system can record and show members' photos and names as they arrive in the club so that you can greet them, and generate reminders and messages depending on the member's status.

As with the simplest card file system described above, the most basic way of identifying members at risk is by monitoring their visit patterns and highlighting fluctuations.

If records show that a member has made no visits to the gym since joining, this indicates a high risk; and a low number of visits is an indicator that a member could become high risk, and needs an intervention. There are a number of ways to calculate low visits, as set out below:

- Simplest: any member who makes fewer than 'x' visits per week

- More complex: consider members who visit less than average for your club, or in a specific group (e.g. age range)

- Smartest: monitor each member's visit pattern; a big reduction in visits makes them high risk

The smartest method ensures that a member who visits regularly once a fortnight is not deemed to be high risk, unless they skip a visit. Whereas a member who visits frequently four times a week becomes high risk if they suddenly start visiting once a week. Regularity (fixed intervals) rather than frequency (often) is the important factor in assessing visits.

Drop out risk

Drop out risk (DOR) is a factor that suggests how likely a member is to 'drop out' or leave the club. It is a number expressed either as a percentage or on a scale from 0-10, where low risk members (0) are the least likely to leave and a higher number indicates there is more risk of the member leaving.

Other factors that some systems take into account when calculating DOR include:

- Length of membership: shorter LoM means DOR is higher, whereas established (long-term members) are less likely to drop out.

- Age: younger members are more likely to drop out than older members.

- Compliance with exercise programme: members who complete 100 per cent of their programme are less likely to drop out than members who underachieve, or over-achieve (i.e. are not challenged by their exercise programme).

- Programme validity: members whose programme has expired have a higher DOR.

- Membership type: different membership types can be categorised as higher risk (one-month memberships are higher risk than eighteen-month, or individual memberships are higher risk than family/couple).

- Postcode: members who live further from the club are more likely to drop out than those who live nearby.

Systems or modules within membership software combine these factors to calculate the DOR of individual members. Their primary use is to identify members who are high risk in order to interact with them to try to reduce their risk. This could be a simple rule to contact anyone with DOR greater than 80 per cent if they are in the club, or in more sophisticated systems, you can identify a large shift in DOR say from 20-60 per cent in a week, and speak to those members first.

As well as speaking to members, DOR can be used to trigger messages; for example, a high risk member might be sent an e-mail or text, particularly if they are absent from the club, and would not otherwise be contacted.

The diagrams below compare different members to show how DOR can be affected by different factors such as visit frequency, age or length of membership. More shading behind the member indicates higher risk of drop-out.

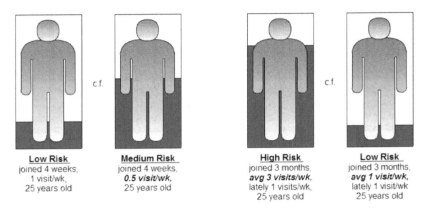

DOR varies with visits or visit trends for new members

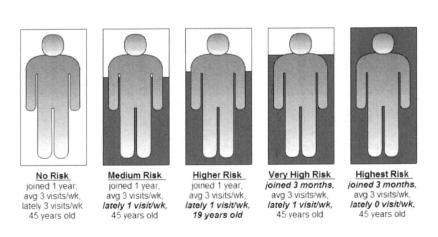

DOR increases with visits, age, newness, etc.

Reducing risk

If you measure risk, then you also need to do something about it. Knowing that DOR changes seasonally is useful, but affecting it is another thing. For the basic measurement, you can only reduce risk by getting members to visit more regularly, which is an excellent intention, since it will also increase retention. More complex equations do not change this practice much; the main aim is to get members visiting regularly, since you cannot do anything to change age or length of membership.

When exercise programme compliance is part of the DOR formula, then the instructor can sometimes affect DOR more directly by reviewing the programme, as illustrated in the following example.

Example: reviewing the exercise programme

A member who is visiting around once a week, only been a member for 3 months, and is completing 6/10 of the exercises on their programme has a DOR of 82 per cent.

The instructor chats to the member about their programme, removes the exercises they don't enjoy (and perhaps adds some more) and as their programme compliance increases to 9/9 exercises, their DOR comes down to 60 per cent. They also start visiting more often, which reduces DOR further.

Retention management systems

With the steady improvements in specifications, and different functions and focuses, it is difficult to compare or recommend certain retention systems or modules. Good retention systems should do one or more of the following three things:

1. Track the member journey.

2. Calculate DOR.

3. Contact absent members.

These are the basics; some systems will cover all areas to different degrees, and have different complexity. For some clubs, a simple system is best; knowing that members receive regular retention e-mails is enough. Others want to configure different risk factors for different postcodes or membership types, and trigger contact reminders for members whose DOR increases by more than 25 per cent over 2 weeks.

Retention Management Systems – In-Club Focus

In terms of in-club member interaction, your retention management system should:

- List members who are currently in the club

- Display member visit (and exercise) history

- Link to front of house system (record visits)

- Provide contact reminders (manual and automatic)

- Record notes/goals from interactions for future reference

Retention Management Systems – External Focus

Looking outside the club, your system should help you to communicate with members who are visiting and those who aren't. You should ensure there are:

- Different message types, based on member/club choice; e-mail, SMS text, letter, etc.

- Welcome and initial journey messages (automated)

- Templates for staff to use to send standard, personalised messages

- Absentee messages (manual/automated)

Retention Management Systems – Reporting

Management and staff should be interested in reports, for example:

- Individual member performance improvements

- Effectiveness of member contacts

- Overall DOR performance

- Member retention, attrition, and so on (see 'Reporting' section in this chapter)

This hub and spoke diagram shows the possible modules and functions of a member retention system. Some systems specialise in different areas, or only perform one function, while others can cover all aspects.

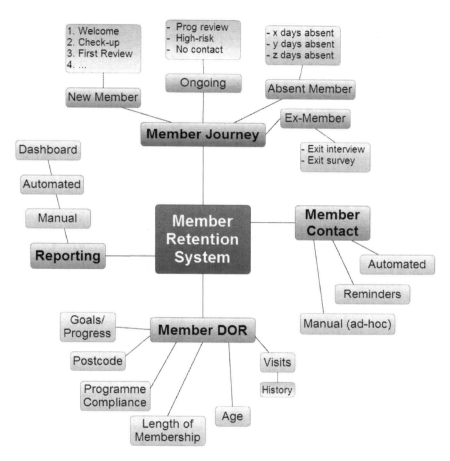

Components of a retention system

Exercise management systems

Compliance with exercise programmes was mentioned when discussing DOR earlier; this is difficult to measure without an exercise management system (EMS), but not impossible. Exercise cards can be regularly monitored, and if your staff are good at data entry, you can record the percentage of workouts completed in a database or spreadsheet. Like the card file system, this is very difficult to scale up once you have hundreds of members.

Technogym, FitLinxx and Pulse offer the three most popular exercise management systems. Their primary purpose is to measure members' workouts, but an EMS also helps to guide members in the gym, and record other activities too. A key, card or pin is entered into each piece of exercise equipment, which recognises the member, advises on the exercise to be performed (time, distance, weight, reps, etc.) and records the results.

Instructors write members' exercise programmes onto the system, and can then track how much of the programme is completed. Typically, a score below 80 per cent means the member is underperforming or the programme is too hard, and a score over 120 per cent means the programme is too easy, or the member is not challenged enough. Completing 100 per cent of the programme on each visit would result in a low DOR, but a completion rate of under 80 per cent or over 120 per cent will cause the DOR to increase.

Exercise management systems offer much more than the facility to record exercises; they can link to heart rate monitors to measure performance index, record biometrics such as BMI (body mass index) or VO2 max (maximal oxygen uptake) to assess members' fitness levels.

It should also be noted that exercise management systems can be inaccurate if used wrongly by members. It may be possible to record all exercises as 'done' when checking out, or members may forget to check out, which can cause problems with the data. This is not down to members 'cheating' the system (they are just cheating themselves), but member education can help address minor issues.

Some manufacturers of EMS recognise the market outside the club too, and have developed devices that record all types of activity, whether it is steps, movement, or heart rate. For the member who wants to log all of their movement, these are great tools, and will improve retention further if there is always a link back to the club.

Club 2.0

Technogym's Club 2.0 or Profile App is proving to be an excellent tool in improving member retention. Each member takes a 2-minute questionnaire, which generates an aspiration map. This tells staff more about the member, in terms of what motivates them to exercise. Technogym's main drivers for the product are exercise programme design for the individual member, and club design using all aspiration maps combined to create a club map.

However, Club 2.0 is also very useful to staff in providing information that helps them to know how to interact with members, as staff know their aspirations; and while they can recommend specific exercises, they can also suggest classes and activities based on aspirations. It is also a useful prospecting and marketing tool, allowing a club to target prospects and members with specific aspiration-based mailings and offers.

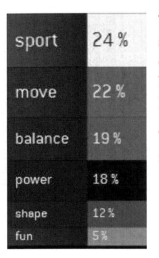

This example Aspiration Map shows someone who is primarily focused on exercising for Sport, but also motivated by Move and partially by Balance and Power.

They place less focus on Fun and Shape in terms of their exercise motivation.

Example of an Aspiration Map created by the Profile App

Reporting

A key part of any retention system is the facility to produce reports. Even in the simplest system described at the start of this chapter, you should record how many members are active each week, and how many become absent. With a measure on new joiners each week, this will build up a trend that you can track and try to affect through your retention initiatives.

Standard retention reports that many clubs use include the 12-month retention, length of membership, and monthly or annual attrition reports. We'll look at definitions of these reports and how to create them in due course.

However, it is sometimes difficult for staff to identify with 12-month retention or attrition reports. Interacting well with 50 members this week is not going to affect the average length of membership, so it is good to have some smaller metrics that can show the short-term effect. It is always much easier to understand data pictorially (charts and graphs) than a table of numbers. The following pages show a few alternative ways of measuring retention initiatives, along with some more 'traditional' retention reports.

Filters and dashboards

It is sometimes important to be able to focus on certain areas in a report, or to filter out unwanted information. Filters can add clarity and reveal a truer picture. For example, looking at certain contract types or certain clubs within a chain can show different variations or highlight trends.

Some systems offer a dashboard view of reports, which usually shows a real-time view of various reports, with or without filters. Just like a car dashboard, which shows your speed, revs, and how much fuel you have left, a club or chain dashboard can show how many members you have gained or lost, how often they are visiting, and drop out risk levels.

New member visit report

Here is a table and chart showing how many members are
'Established' (longer than 4 weeks) or 'New', and how many of
those have visited in the last 4 weeks. This can be recorded at the
start of each month, and targets set to improve the numbers. For
example, the New Absent members were at 2 per cent last
month, and are now down to 1 per cent, which is great!

New members more active than last month

	Members	Percentage	Change
Established	825	66%	+1%
Absent	311	25%	
New	95	8%	
New Absent	12	1%	-1%
Total	**1,243**		

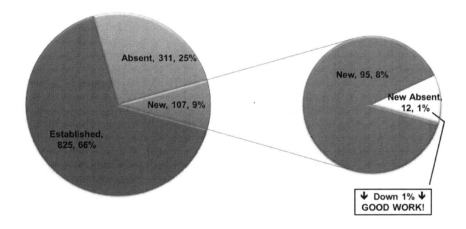

Total Member count, segmented by active status and new-ness

Programme or visit status

This report is very versatile in that it could show many different metrics or comparisons. The basic premise is to show who or what is performing well, perhaps create some competition, and raise the game.

The example in the chart below shows the percentage of each group that have a valid exercise programme, compared with those who expired recently, or longer ago. The x axis shows instructors, but could equally well portray different sites, contract type, age ranges, membership lengths, and so on. Diana is the most effective at keeping members on a current programme, with Peter in second place.

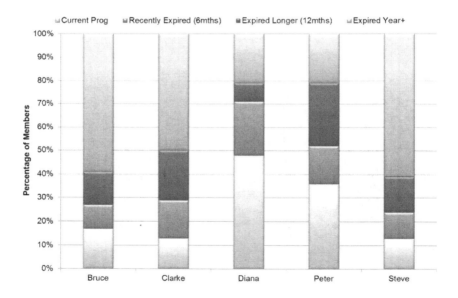

Member programme validity by staff member

Following this report, the target was set for everyone to achieve the same state as Diana as a minimum, that is, at least 50 per cent of members should be on a valid exercise programme.

Rather than programme 'validity', this report could equally show visit status, how many members have goals, or simply how many have an interaction recorded in recent times.

Interaction effectiveness

This chart shows how many members have been contacted in the previous month, and what effect those contacts are having on the members on average. A member who visits 2 times per week prior to contact, and subsequently visits 3 times is seen as a 50 per cent increase in visit frequency.

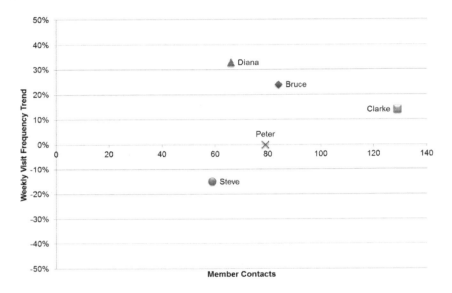

Number of members contacted, and effect on visits

Clarke contacted the most members last month, and is having a good effect, but Diana's and Bruce's members are showing an increase in the number of visits they make. Steve needs to 'pull his socks up' in terms of members contacted and effect.

Membership decay

A decay graph is a real-time retention curve in reverse. It shows the proportion of people who joined each month that are still members today.

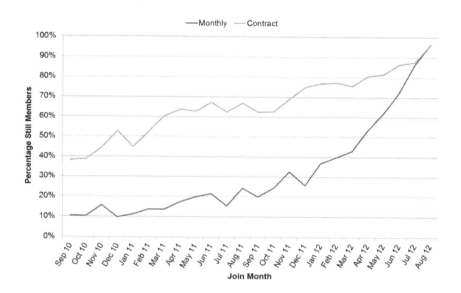

Proportion of memberships live vs. cancelled

(recorded at start of Sept 2012)

This report is great for comparing different clubs, member groups or, in this case, contract types. The steep decline for 'Monthly' is symptomatic of the club's offering. At this club, monthly contracts are priced accordingly, and monthly members are also contacted more regularly to try to improve the curve, that is, get a larger proportion of them to remain members longer.

Member retention

The definition of member retention used by ukactive (formerly the Fitness Industry Association) is 'the proportion of members who retain their membership for any predetermined time period e.g. three, six or twelve months'.

The retention graph below shows the expected retention rate at a club with two different membership types, if membership cancellation were not an option.

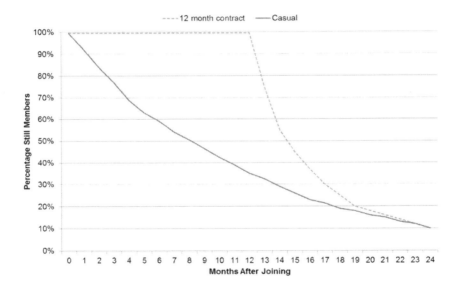

Expected retention chart for different contract options

Twelve-month retention is a classic measure, and the fitness industry average is typically quoted at around 65 per cent. This means that 65 per cent of members stay for at least 12 months, or to put it another way, 35 per cent of members have left by month 12 of their membership. Twelve-month retention varies widely, based on club type (premium, trust, local authority, budget, etc.), membership type (contract), location, and a variety of other factors.

The graph below shows actual retention rate for three different contract types at a club. Initially, contract 1 performs best, but by month 12, it has the lowest value, and drops further at month 13. Contract 2 performs best after month 3, and looks like it brings in the most revenue. Revenue can be calculated as the area under the line multiplied by the membership fee.

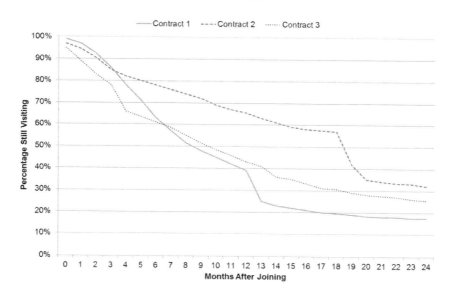

Real retention chart for group of clubs

(based on last visit date, rather than last paid date)

Putting revenue and contract length aside for a moment, it is often interesting to measure retention in terms of the last visit date, rather than the last 'paid' date. The 12-month 'retention' will undoubtedly be lower, this will be reflected in the graph, but you will know how long your members stay for, on average. This is explored in more detail in the following pages.

Length of membership

Like 12-month retention, length of membership (LoM) is a long-term metric, which can be evaluated quarterly or annually but is unlikely to change significantly in the short term.

The ukactive definition of length of membership is 'the median (average) length of membership in months'.

New members who joined in the previous month will have a maximum membership length of 1 month, so if you have a lot of members who have recently joined, these can bring your average LoM down. You could exclude members who joined in the last 12 months, or take those into account and compare like for like.

In the chart below, two different contract types are compared for length of membership, and whether members had recorded an exercise goal. Members with recorded goals stay much longer than those without, so all instructors were then encouraged to talk to members and record their goals in the system.

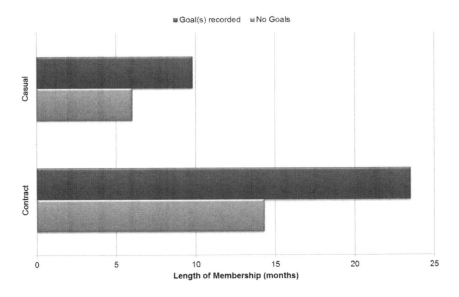

LoM for different contracts and goal status

Attrition rate

Attrition rate is defined by ukactive as 'the average number of members per thousand who cancel every month'.

Compared with retention or length of membership, attrition is a good ongoing measure that can be targeted each month. A month of high membership sales can bring attrition down, as can be seen from the January and February figures in the table below.

Comparison of attrition rates between clubs belonging to a chain

	Club A	Club B	Club C	Club D	Club E	Total
Jul	13.9%	5.7%	9.9%	14.7%	10.7%	9.8%
Aug	11.8%	10.4%	15.1%	14.3%	12.7%	10.9%
Sep	16.5%	6.1%	4.8%	10.8%	8.4%	8.4%
Oct	12.2%	7.8%	8.2%	9.9%	9.4%	9.2%
Nov	10.6%	5.2%	7.3%	10.4%	8.5%	7.5%
Dec	11.9%	6.5%	8.4%	11.2%	9.8%	8.8%
Jan	9.8%	5.5%	7.2%	10.7%	7.5%	7.8%
Feb	7.8%	4.0%	5.6%	7.3%	6.0%	6.8%
Mar	14.9%	8.4%	13.8%	12.5%	12.8%	12.2%
Apr	7.4%	4.4%	6.3%	6.3%	6.7%	6.0%
May	11.7%	8.3%	10.9%	9.2%	12.2%	9.3%
Jun	15.9%	10.1%	14.8%	12.3%	14.2%	12.2%

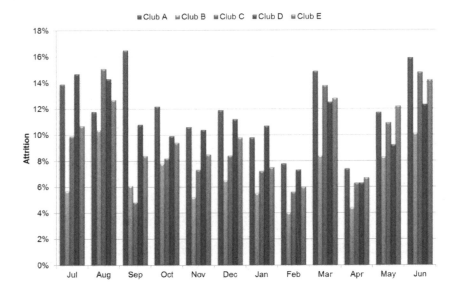

Graph to show attrition for a chain of 5 clubs

Club A shows the highest attrition in general, consistently higher than average every month. Clubs C and E, and occasionally D also have high attrition, whereas Club B is consistently low.

Risk of leaving

This report shows when ex-members make their last visit. There is often a clear peak around month 3, regardless of contract but some clubs have a higher peak in month 1 or 2, showing more serious problems in early membership.

Timely contact can help to reduce drop out, or you may want to design or review your member journey based on your version of this chart.

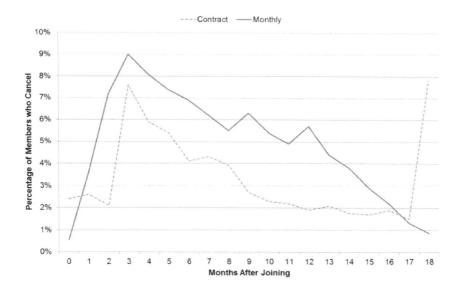

Monthly risk highest at month 3 for both contract types

Risk of leaving can be attributed to several factors, from contract length to lack of engagement, or poorly designed member journey. Decide what you can affect, and take action to try to reduce the risk peaks.

Membership growth

This dual axis chart shows the total number of paying members (left axis), and the number of members joining and leaving each month (right axis). Although sales remain fairly constant, it is clear that member retention is a problem, as the leavers column is growing, and the total members' line is in decline from the start of 2012.

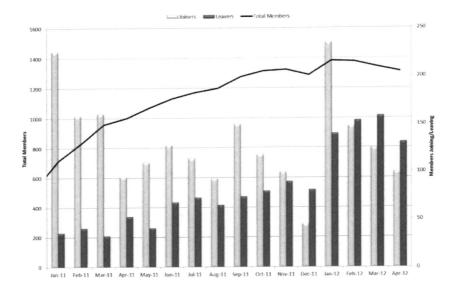

Total joiners/leavers, and growth of membership

This chart is a good 'eye-opener' to realising a retention problem; you could then use other measures to identify where the problem lies (e.g. risk of leaving) and try to affect the leavers.

Member churn

The following chart shows how many joiners each month have a previous membership. An ex-member campaign in May 2011 triggered lots of churning members in June 2011, as well as many referrals for new members!

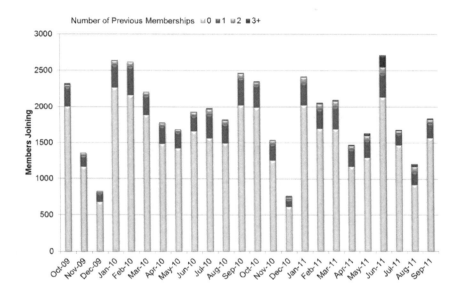

Member Churn

Total members joining each month, showing how many had a number of previous memberships

Summary/Actions

☐ Keep It Simple (Stupid).

☐ Processes and understanding are the system.

☐ Drop Out Risk (DOR) helps identify members who could leave; your job is to reduce DOR.

☐ Use Retention Systems to

1. Track the member journey

2. Calculate DOR

3. Contact absent members

☐ Use reports to inform, react and change your retention policy or journey.

10. Conclusion

People, systems and communications

If you are an audiophile, you will know that a good separates system comprises three key components: source (turntable, CD, MP3 player, etc), amplifier, and speakers. If you have all three in balance, you will have a good sound, and listening pleasure. Spending too much on speakers is pointless if you have a poor source or amplifier. The principle of managing the three cornerstones of gym membership retention is similar.

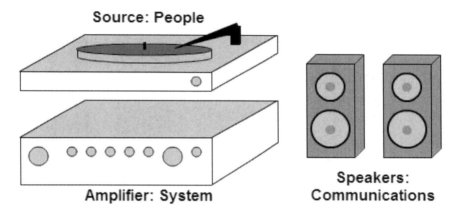

A good separates system comprises three components

Think of your people as the source, your systems as the amplifier, and your communications as the speakers. Spending time and money, or focusing equally on each will achieve the best results. Investing heavily in communications without a system is unlikely to give great results. Some low-cost gyms focus on system and communications without people, much like an amplifier with a built in tuner, and speakers. This will play music, but you are limiting the potential of your system.

KPIs

Measuring the effect of your retention initiatives is really important if you want to improve your performance. Targets can really help too, if you know where you are now, and where you want to get to. High-level retention or attrition metrics can provide management with the information they want, but it is also important to have day-to-day initiatives and targets that the gym team can work towards, which will help to build the big picture.

Take up to 5 Key Performance Indicators (KPIs) that your club is working towards, and build them into your daily, weekly, or monthly processes. Measure the team and the individual's contribution to member retention. If everyone in your club is aligned and working towards these goals, you should be able to hit the targets you've set.

Examples of 10 KPIs

1. Talk to <*x*> % of your high risk members each week.

2. Maintain at least <*x*> % active members per month.

3. Ensure a minimum of <*x*> % complete your new member journey.

4. Reduce attrition from last month.

5. Increase 12-month retention by <*x*> % 6 months from now.

6. Offer a review to <*x*> % of members every month.

7. Praise <*x*> members on completing their goal each week.

8. Get in touch with <*x*> % of lapsed members each month. (Speak to them, messages don't count!).

9. Engage <*x*> members in a challenge each month.

10. Convince <*x*> members to join a class or visit a free class.

Change

If you're going to improve your member retention, then you are almost certainly going to have to make some changes. Not all staff (or members) will welcome changes, but you won't be able to progress otherwise. Remember the change formula from the introduction? If you haven't been able to work it out yet, here's the solution:

If you're looking to make a change in your club or in anything else in business or life, it is worth bearing in mind the change formula:

Change happens when

$$Co\ (SQ) > R\ (C)$$

The **Co**st of the **S**tatus **Q**uo

is **greater than**

the **R**isk of **C**hange

In other words, until the cost of the status quo increases, or the risk diminishes, change will not happen. Think about the cost of staying where you are, and balance it with the risk of changing. Sometimes we replace risk with resistance, although they are usually related.

Change Formula by Alan M Webber
@alanmwebber
www.rulesofthumbbook.com

Finally, remember that people don't join a health club wanting to leave. If you can keep your members feeling the way they do when they join, they won't want to leave. It's simple, but it's not easy!

Hopefully, some of the tips and practices in this book will help you to get your members to stick around.

For additional online resources, diagrams, videos and support material go to www.ggfit.com/stickaround/extras

Annex 1: Summary lists

Retention tips for instructors

Interaction

1. *Learn* a new member's name every day – introduce yourself.

2. *Smile and greet* everyone within 3 metres (members and staff).

3. *Ask* your members questions– find out about them.

4. *Listen* to their answers; learn about your members (they're the experts, not you!).

Goals

5. Ensure members take *responsibility* for their goals.

6. Help them to push themselves to get the *results* they want.

7. Give members what *they* want (within reason).

You

8. You are paid by the members, not by the club (without members, there is no club).

9. Practice what you preach; know your own goals, and work towards them every day.

10. Share your retention ideas with colleagues and management.

Retention tips for management

People

1. *Lead* by example – see specific items on above list.

2. *Walk* the gym floor every day, *talk* (and *listen*) to members too.

3. *Feedback* positive and negative comments and *listen* to staff.

Journey, goals, mantras

4. *Know* the member journey, sell it to staff, and help them to sell it to members too.

5. Know the personal goals of your staff, share yours with them.

6. The customer is not always right (not when they make staff unhappy, are bad for business, or get unfair advantage).

Communication and systems

7. Be clear on the member communication process; when do members receive messages and how effective are they?

8. Have the most recent KPIs to hand, and know the trend.

9. Be innovative; try new things, and monitor the success.

10. Balance your retention focus on people, communication and systems. When one part is working well, improve it, if another component is not working, change it.

Top ten retention tips

1. Ask for member feedback; request it regularly, publish results and act on them.

2. Treat each member as an individual.

3. Have a standard member journey, but be able to adapt.

4. Use all communication channels available to you.

5. Make sure members get results; reward them when they do.

6. Get absent members back.

7. Communicate with ex-members.

8. Undersell, over deliver: exceed expectations.

9. Monitor your retention efforts; understand what works.

10. Better staff retention leads to better member retention.

Annex 2: Club messages

The following messages are a resource for clubs to use or mix and match to communicate with members.

Each message can be combined along with news and events to make a monthly member newsletter, or regular ex-member communications and prospect offers.

They could be sent via:

- ☐ e-mail

- ☐ SMS text (watch out for message length)

- ☐ letters (in the post)

- ☐ social media such as Facebook or Twitter.

Systems such as Technogym's Contact Manager, Communicator, or Cascade[3d]'s tools help to tailor bespoke messages, or you can use conventional mailing solutions such as MailChimp or DotMailer.

Before you start

Be prepared to receive and deal with members' replies and responses.

1. Ensure all staff know which messages have been sent, why, and how.

2. Make sure member replies are received, particularly e-mails and texts.

3. Handle responses, both in the club and if a member replies in writing.

4. Change the messages regularly to keep members interested, and combine messages for maximum effect.

Some Dos and Don'ts

1. If a member asks about a message or returns from absence saying 'I got this message', don't say 'Really?' Use it as an opportunity to re-engage with the member and help them with what they want/need.

2. When sending absence messages, include the latest offer/challenge, as an absent member will not have heard about this in the club.

3. Try to always include a 'What's In It for Me?' WIIFM (or member) in your message. This ensures more opens/reads/effectiveness.

4. When sending e-mails, the text in the subject line controls whether the member opens the message. Make the subject line relevant and attention grabbing.

5. Use form fields where possible to personalise messages. For example, Dear *<name>*, from *<trainer>*, at *<club>*, a bonus *<gift>*.

6. Differentiate between marketing messages (e.g. newsletters) which members can unsubscribe from, and reminder messages, which help them to stay motivated.

New member messages

Welcoming and encouraging new members is incredibly important. This is the time when many members need extra attention, and also presents a good opportunity to check for marketing permission. Open up the communication channels now and they will receive and read messages going forward, particularly if you get the WIIFM right.

Thank you for joining

As a new member we would like to welcome you to our club. Don't forget to book your <first review session> before you leave today.

All new joiners get this message within 2-3 days to encourage them to stick to the member journey

Congratulations, you have completed your first month

You have done it! To show how proud we are, you can collect a <complimentary guest pass to bring a friend for free>. See the fitness team to collect yours.

This message is sent at the end of the member's first month to praise and to encourage use of a friend for motivation, retention and referral.

Time for a review?

It's been <n> days/months since you first joined <club>. Keep your fitness and motivation levels up with an exercise programme review with <trainer> or any other instructors next time you're in the club.

This message checks that members are still on the journey and promotes the review.

Ongoing messages / promotions

Running regular promotions keeps members interested, especially if there's a WIIFM. If you don't mention all of them in your monthly newsletter, ensure they are posted on the website, noticeboards, Communicator, or the club window.

Friend for free Friday

Don't forget that on Friday this week you can bring a friend for free. To bring your friend, simply collect a voucher before you leave today and bring both your friend and your voucher on Friday.

This message is sent up to a week before the following Friday. The voucher can be a simple data capture sheet that the member's friend will need to gain entry. It helps retention and referral.

Workmate wellness

If you work locally then maybe you and your colleagues could benefit from our corporate arrangements. Drop your business card at reception and let us do the rest.

This message goes out once every 2-3 months to get members who work locally to introduce their team. This is an excellent way into new corporate opportunities.

Would you like 1 month's free membership?

If the answer is 'yes' then don't forget to refer a friend to join this month. The more friends you introduce the more free months you will receive. Referral cards are held at reception.

This is a direct request and pay-off for referring new members. This should encourage referrals and persuade members to bring their friends into the gym throughout the month.

Open weekend

We're holding an Open Weekend from Friday <date> to Sunday <date>, so make sure you bring your family and friends down for a class, workout, swim, or treatment. Don't forget that you can get an extra month's free membership for yourself for any friends that take out a membership.

This is a reminder that there will be guests in at the weekend (better to tell members direct than for them to see the banner) and that they can benefit too!

Seminar season

During <month> our instructors will be holding weekly seminars on topics ranging from diet to weight loss to increasing strength.

If you would like to attend our first session this <day> at <time>pm on <relaxation and back care> please book your place now. Friends and non-members are welcome to join you.

This message allows the opportunity for PT promotion, increases the perceived value to the membership and provides a great referral opportunity. Weekly seminars give the chance for different groups of people to attend.

What makes you move?

Have you completed your aspiration map yet? Ask a member of the gym team to run through the 2-minute questionnaire that will show your exercise aspirations and help with your programming.

Sells the benefits of aspirational maps and tailored programmes, adding value to membership.

Seasonal messages / promotions

Seasonal messages should also be published on every bulletin board available, and can work well to bring in new prospects and member guests.

Valentine's Vitality (February)

Look trim and toned for that special someone; prepare for the chocolates and champagne, or be on the lookout for love at our special Valentine Vitality (VV) classes. All VV classes running for the next two weeks include a voucher for a free drink at the bar/café/lounge, so flirt in your class and meet up for a chat after – get those heart rates rising!

This is for anyone who needs a little extra motivation; get the instructors to create the atmosphere, do some match-making and encourage everyone to the bar!

Easter Eggsercise

Beat the Easter Bunny with our Easter Eggstravaganza. We are putting on bonus classes and free taster sessions to help you to balance the chocolate scales. Why not try something new or review your fitness goals or targets?

This targets January joiners during the 3-4 month high drop-out phase, but is also a great way of readdressing those New Year's resolutions that may have gone awry.

Bikini body/Speedo sessions (May-June)

Do you want to look great on the beach this summer? Then sign-up for our bikini body and Speedo sessions and really focus on your shape over the next 10 weeks. Set personal targets with one of our instructors, and if you achieve your goal, we'll give you an extra bonus <details of bonus>.

This reminds a lot of members why they joined the gym, re-engages and focuses them before their holidays.

It's Halloween time! (October)

To celebrate we are holding our special Halloween Open Weekend. With ghostly classes, scarily good taster sessions and treats throughout the club, you can bring your friends for free all weekend. To book your friend in, ask at reception now.

This adds more value to your members' experience, encourages referrals and adds an element of fun to any ordinary weekend.

Give the gift of health (December)

Do you know someone who needs that extra push to get fitter, or are you looking to help a friend or loved one to be healthier? Buy them the Gift of Health: <n> month's membership for just <price>. It's one of our most popular promotions, only available until 31 December.

This is not usually a 'surprise' gift, but really is a successful promotion at several clubs. Giving health and fitness as a gift shows that you really care about someone. Also, we often see Pay&Play members buying this gift for themselves and partners.

Challenges

Holding regular challenges gives your members a little extra motivation to achieve a goal, compete with each other, or just see personal improvements from the start to the finish of the challenge, or from year to year. Large charts or graphs positioned on the gym wall showing results of challenges provide a good opportunity for members to see how they are performing.

Rowing ladder

Simple distance rowing challenge; this could be ongoing with different distances each month.

Most calories

This challenge may be easily monitored with an exercise management system, or can be simply calculated with time, weight and equipment. (See also, 'Best moves' below.)

Iron pumped

As above, but resistance based.

Distance travelled / marathon

Run or cycle a set distance in the lead up to national events (London Marathon, Tour de France, etc.).

Triathlon

Row/Step, then Cycle, then Run specific distances, with the cumulative time measured to calculate winners.

Olympics

Triathlon (normally Swim, Cycle, Run), combines three disciplines to complete.

Heptathlon (normally 100 m hurdles, high jump, shot put, 200 m, long jump, javelin, 800 m) combines up to eight disciplines to complete

Decathlon (100 m, long jump, shot put, high jump, 400 m, 110 m hurdles, discus, pole vault, javelin, 1,500 m) combines up to 10 exercises to complete

Winter Olympics

As above, focused on exercises to improve ski/snowboard/ skating techniques.

World Cup

Run further than Rooney/Ronaldinho/other. Choose a footballer, and see if you can cover the same weekly distance that they do in all their tournament matches.

Top of the classes

Offer a prize to the person who attends the most classes or more than <x> classes in a week, or month. This may include a free class for the winner, 5 free guest passes, a whole free class for the winner's friends (members and non-members), or a t-shirt – the 'yellow jersey' of classes.

Best moves

For members with a club pedometer, FitLinxx pebble, or Technogym mywellness key; the member who has achieved the most moves or biggest percentage of their target each month can be proclaimed the winner. 'Moves' can work better as a challenge than 'calories', as it offers a more even playing field between men and women, for example.

The winner will probably be very pleased already, so a 'prize' may be unnecessary, as the results they are achieving are motivational. In this case, it is often better to make them member of the month, display their photo and story on the club noticeboard, or in the newsletter.

Most visits

For the keen, but gentle exerciser, a challenge based on the most visits can be a great competition. It is also useful in helping new members to get into the exercise habit. Produce a prize, or display names of members who have hit the target of <x> visits per month, or in their first month. Sign up new members to this challenge as they join.

All in the name of charity

Hold an event such as a triathlon in aid of a named charity. Offer a weekly circuit class and fitness tips to enable participants to prepare for the event. Ensure that sponsorship forms are available at the gym and encourage non-members to take part.

This opportunity allows members to train towards a new goal with the support of a PT to upsell this area. It also allows members to include friends and, more importantly, allows the clubs and its members to put something of value back into their community or chosen charity.

Corporate challenge

Challenge corporate members to create teams of five participants, three of whom should be club members to compete against other corporate teams; activities could include running, cycling and rowing.

The total focus of this challenge is on getting corporate members to bring along friends and colleagues to the gym. Non-members are welcome to make up the team so adds to referrals, as well as retention-based fitness challenge.

Absent member messages

Use tools such as Technogym's Contact Manager, Retention Management, Cascade 3d or your front of house system to know when members are high risk, or have not visited for some time.

Personalisation is important for these messages, as is variety (e-mail one week, followed by a text or phone call). Combine absence messages with fitness tips and promotions/offers.

Examples of text to include in messages sent to absentees are given here.

> Dear *<name>*
>
> We notice you've not been to *<club>* lately. We want to help you move towards your exercise goals, so get back in soon and let our instructors know if you need any extra motivation; they're here to help.
>
> Where have you been? We miss you. Come back to *<club>* to get your exercise back on track, perhaps a programme review or check on your aspirations.
>
> Where have you been? We want you back. Why not book in for an exercise programme or goal review when you come back.
>
> It looks like you've not been to *<club>* for a few weeks. We hope you'll come back soon; our team are waiting for you.
>
> According to our records, you've not been to *<club>* for *<x>* weeks now. Come back soon to keep up the exercise habit.
>
> We've missed you down at *<club>*. What can we do to get you back into the exercise habit?
>
> Have you been on holiday? We've not seen you for a while. We're looking forward to seeing you again; come back soon!
>
> It seems you've been busy lately, but not down at *<club>*. Make time for exercise by reviewing your goals with one of our instructors next time you're in.

Did we say/do something wrong, as we've not seen you for a while? Have a chat with *<trainer>* or any other instructor for some extra motivation or new exercises.

We've not seen you much lately. We are *<club mantra here>*, so why not come and join in a class *<link to timetable>*.

A break is a good as a rest. Regular exercise is addictive. Don't break the habit; it's a good one

Remember how you felt after your last workout? Get down to *<club>* and get that feeling again.

Sometimes it's difficult to work up to making the next visit, but you know it will be worth it.

If you're thinking of dropping out, we're not going to let you! Keep regular to keep fit.

Get yourself back down to *<club>* soon, or all that good work you've put in will go to waste.

The longer you leave it, the harder it will be to get back on track with your fitness.

You've never going to achieve your fitness goals if you don't visit *<club>*.

Come back to *<club>* before it's too late.

Get back or get fat.*

---

* This is included as a 'jokey' suggestion made by an instructor in a workshop. It shows the importance of using standard corporate templates, but might also generate ideas or more suggestions.

Examples of questions used in surveys

Surveys are a useful way of keeping in touch with all contacts on your database, particularly ex-members. The key driver for carrying out surveys is not always to find out the answers to the questions but to stay in touch with ex-members and show you still value their opinion. The questions you ask can sometimes steer ex-members towards re-joining.

Here are some examples of questions already used in member surveys.

Question	Response
<Club> provides everything that was promised when I joined.	Yes/Maybe/No
<Club> has a friendly atmosphere.	Totally/ Sometimes/ Not often/ Not at all
I always feel safe when using a *<club>* Gym	Yes/ Sometimes/ Not often/ No
Staff are available to provide free advice when I need help.	Always/Sometimes/ Not often/ Never
Staff are approachable and helpful.	Always/Sometimes/ Not often/ Never
I know the name of at least 1 member of the staff team.	Yes/ No
Who has helped motivate you in the gym most this month?	*<list of trainers>*
<Club> has all the facilities I need.	Yes/ Maybe/ No
<Club> emails me with advice and information.	Too often/ Enough/ Not enough/ Never

The monthly gym price is excellent value for money.	Yes/ Maybe/ No
<Club> is helping me become a healthier person.	Totally/ Sometimes/ Not often/ Not at all
How likely are you to recommend *<club>* to a friend?	(Where 0 is not likely and 10 is definitely)
How likely are you to be a member of *<club>* in 6 months' time?	(Where 0 is not likely and 10 is extremely likely)
Have you paid for a personal training session since joining *<club>*?	Yes/No

Annex 3: the total member journey

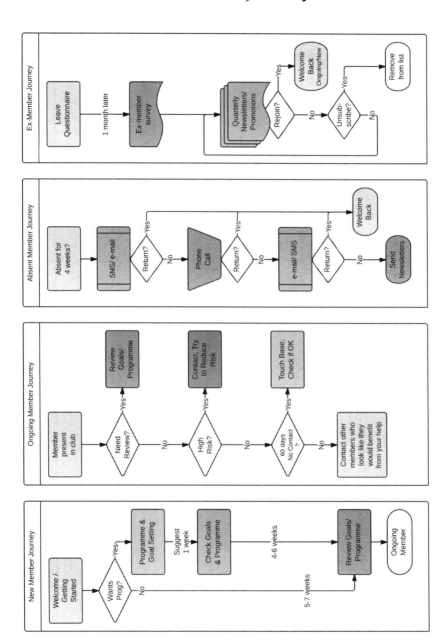

Websites: Retention Systems

www.cascade3d.com

Cascade3d – Reporting and Communicate

---

www.fitlinxx.com

FitLinxx – Professional – Exercise Management System

---

www.retentionmanagement.com

Retention Management – automated e-mail, sms & social media

---

www.ggfit.com

Retention Consultancy – help and advice on all the systems here

---

www.technogym.com

Technogym – Wellness System, Contact Manager, Cloud Apps

---

www.theretentionpeople.com

The Retention People / Fitronics – Retention software & training

---

Bibliography

Gerson, Richard (1999), *Members for Life: Proven Service and Retention Strategies for Health-fitness and Sports Clubs*, Human Kinetics

Hillsdon, Melvyn and Paul Bedford (2008), *An Expert Guide to Retention and Attrition,* Fitness Industry Association (now ukactive)

Webber, Alan (1999), *Rules of Thumb: 52 Principles for Winning at Business without Losing Your Self,* USA, Harper Collins/Harper Business

Diagrams

Index

About the author

Guy Griffiths describes himself as a Fitness Industry Revolution Consultant. He is still relatively new to the fitness industry, compared to some seasoned professionals. Therefore he looks to question the status quo, help to facilitate change, and share and spread the word on member-retention initiatives that work.

He grew up in Northampton with his parents and two younger sisters. He still meets regularly with school friends, and measures his worth by his friendships and relationships.

Guy studied Aeronautics and Astronautics at the University of Southampton, achieving a B. Eng (Hons) 2:1 degree, finishing in the top 10 per cent of his year. He worked at British Airways as part of an industrial placement year, but turned away from engineering in favour of a career start in the City of London. Whilst at University, Guy enjoyed playing for the Southampton Skunks Ultimate Frisbee team, his height and speed made him a natural in the end-zone or stack. Visits to the gyms at university and the BA Concorde Centre kept his fitness levels up.

In 1997, Guy joined SMA Financial as a consultant. Tasks included installing and linking banking systems, running technical training courses, promoting and selling resilience, reporting and anti-money-laundering systems. Roles as Education Manager, Consultancy Manager, then Director of Sales and Marketing followed. Guy switched gyms as positions and exercise patterns changed. He also took up running along the banks of the Thames, and participated in charity 10k events for the British Heart Foundation.

Guy left the City to form GG Fit Ltd in 2008. He trained as a life coach to help individuals and businesses realise their goals. His own goal is to positively affect the health and fitness of more people each year. Although he is a keen gym goer, he recognises that it is not such a motivating place for everyone. He believes that working with clubs is the best way to positively affect as many people as possible, and has the added bonus of improving each club's financials.

Guy now spends his time defining retention policy, running interaction coaching workshops for staff, configuring member communication systems, and analysing data for clubs.

When he is not busy increasing the length of memberships at health clubs, Guy is usually working out or swimming in the club. Otherwise, he can be found running, snowboarding, or golfing with friends or spending time with his wife, daughter and son.

Guy's gym memberships

- Southampton University
- BA Concorde Club
- Hampton Pool
- Latchmere Leisure Centre
- Kings College Gym

- Cannons London Bridge
- 37 Degrees London Bridge
- Park Road Leisure Centre
- Carnival Pool
- Power of Pilates
- Park Run (Reading)

Printed and bound by CPI Group (UK) Ltd, Croydon, CR0 4YY

30/03/2024

03756466-0001